Anonymous

Constitution of the M.W. Grand Lodge of Free and Accepted Masons of the State of Nevada,

and by-laws of Elko Lodge, no.15, together with the ancient charges, the

twenty-five landmarks of freemasonry, and a funeral service

Anonymous

Constitution of the M.W. Grand Lodge of Free and Accepted Masons of the State of Nevada,
and by-laws of Elko Lodge, no.15, together with the ancient charges, the twenty-five landmarks of freemasonry, and a funeral service

ISBN/EAN: 9783337115340

Printed in Europe, USA, Canada, Australia, Japan

Cover: Foto ©ninafisch / pixelio.de

More available books at **www.hansebooks.com**

OF THE

M∴ W∴ GRAND LODGE

OF

FREE AND ACCEPTED MASONS OF THE

STATE OF NEVADA,

AND

BY-LAWS OF

Elko Lodge, No. 15,

TOGETHER WITH

THE ANCIENT CHARGES,

THE TWENTY-FIVE LANDMARKS OF FREEMASONRY,

AND A

FUNERAL SERVICE.

CHICAGO:

J. W. MIDDLETON, STATIONER AND STEAM PRINTER,
6 & 7 EAST RANDOLPH STREET.

1872.

Charges of a Freemason,

Extracted from the Ancient Records of Lodges beyond sea, and of those in England, Scotland, and Ireland, for the use of the Lodges in London. To be read at the making of New Brethren, or when the Master shall order it.*

THE GENERAL HEADS, viz :—

I. OF GOD and RELIGION. .
II. Of the CIVIL MAGISTRATE, Supreme and Subordinate.
III. Of LODGES.
IV. Of MASTERS, WARDENS, FELLOWS, and APPRENTICES.
V. Of the Management of the CRAFT in working.
VI. Of BEHAVIOR, viz:—
1. In the Lodge while CONSTITUTED.
2. After the Lodge is over and the BRETHREN not gone.
3. When Brethren meet without STRANGERS, but not in a Lodge.
4. In presence of STRANGERS NOT MASONS.
5. At HOME and in the NEIGHBORHOOD.
6. Toward a STRANGE BROTHER.

I. CONCERNING GOD AND RELIGION.

A Mason is obliged, by his tenure, to obey the moral law ; and if he rightly understands the art, he will never be a stupid atheist nor an irreligious libertine. But though in ancient times Masons were charged in every country to be of the religion of that country or nation, whatever it was, it is now thought more expedient only to oblige them to that religion in which all men agree, leaving their particular opinions to themselves ; that is, to be *good men and true*, or men of honor and honesty, by whatever denominations or persuasions they may be distinguished ; (whereby Masonry

---

* These charges were prepared and presented to the Grand Lodge of Engla nd in 1721 by DR. ANDERSON and DR. DESAGULIERS, and having been approved by the Grand Lodge on the twenty-fifth of March, 1722, were published in the first edition of the Book of Constitutions. They have always been held in the highest veneration by the fraternity, as embodying the most important points of the ancient *written*, as well as unwritten, law of Masonry.

becomes the center of union,) and the means of conciliating true friendship among persons that must have remained at a perpetual distance.

II. OF THE CIVIL MAGISTRATE, SUPREME AND SUBORDINATE.

A Mason is a peaceable subject to the civil powers wherever he resides or works, and is never to be concerned in plots and conspiracies against the peace and welfare of the nation, nor to behave himself undutifully to inferior magistrates; for as Masonry hath always been injured by war, bloodshed, and confusion, so ancient kings and princes have been much disposed to encourage the craftsmen, because of their peaceableness and loyalty, whereby they practically answered the cavils of their adversaries, and promoted the honor of the fraternity, who ever flourished in times of peace: So that if a brother should be a rebel against the state, he is not to be countenanced in his rebellion, however he may be pitied as an unhappy man; and, if convicted of no other crime, though the loyal brotherhood must and ought to disown his rebellion, and give no umbrage or ground of political jealousy to the government for the time being, they can not expel him from the Lodge, and his relation to it remains indefeasible.

III. OF LODGES.

A Lodge is a place where Masons assemble and work; hence that assembly, or duly organized society of Masons, is called a *Lodge*, and every brother ought to belong to one, and to be subject to its by-laws and the General Regulations. It is either particular or general, and will be best understood by attending it, and by the regulations of the General or Grand Lodge hereunto annexed. In ancient times, no Master or Fellow could be absent from it, especially when warned to appear at it, without incurring a severe censure, until it appeared to the Master and Wardens that pure necessity hindered him.

The persons admitted members of a Lodge must be good and true men, free-born, and of mature and discreet age, no bond-men, no women, no immoral or scandalous men, but of good report.

IV. OF MASTERS, WARDENS, FELLOWS, AND APPRENTICES.

All preferment among Masons is grounded upon real worth and personal merit only; that so the lords may be well served, the brethren not put to shame, nor the Royal Craft despised: Therefore no Master or Warden is chosen by seniority, but for his merit. It is impossible to describe these things in writing, and every brother must attend in his place, and learn them in a way peculiar to this fraternity; only candidates may know that no Master should take an Apprentice unless he has sufficient employment for him, and unless he be a perfect youth, having no maim or defect in his body, that may render him uncapable of learning the art of serving his Master's Lord, and of being made a *Brother*, and then a *Fellow Craft* in due time, even after he has served such a term of years as the custom of the country directs; and that he should be descended of honest parents; that so, when otherwise qualified, he may arrive at the honor of being the *Warden*, and then the *Master* of the Lodge, the *Grand Warden*, and at length the *Grand Master* of all the Lodges, according to his merit.

No brother can be a Warden until he has passed the part of a Fellow Craft; nor a Master until he has acted as a Warden, nor Grand Warden until he has been Master of a Lodge, nor Grand Master unless he has been a fellow Craft before his election, who is also to be nobly born, or a gentlemen of the best fashion, or some eminent scholar, or some curious architect, or other artist, descended of honest parents, and who is of singular great merit in the opinion of the Lodges. And for the better, and easier, and more honorable discharge of his office, the Grand Master has a power to choose his own Deputy Grand Master, who must be then, or must have been formerly, the Master of a particular Lodge, and has the privilege of acting whatever the Grand Master, his principal, should act, unless the said principal be present, or interpose his authority by a letter.

These rulers and governors, supreme and subordinate, of the ancient Lodge, are to be obeyed in their respective stations by all the brethren, according to the Old Charges and regulations, with all humility, reverence love and alacrity.

V. OF THE MANAGEMENT OF THE CRAFT IN WORKING.

All Masons shall work honestly on working days, that they may live creditably on holy days; and the time appointed by the law of the land, or confirmed by custom, shall be observed.

The most expert of the Fellow Craftsmen shall be chosen or appointed the Master, or Overseer, of the lord's work; who is to be called *Master* by those that work under him. The Craftsmen are to avoid all ill language, and to call each other by no disobliging name, but brother or fellow; and to behave themselves courteously within and without the Lodge.

The Master knowing himslf to be able of cunning, shall undertake the lord's work as reasonably as possible, and truly dispend his goods as if they were his own; nor to give more wages to any brother or apprentice than he really may deserve.

Both the Master and the Masons receiving their wages justly, shall be faithful to the lord, and honestly finish their work, whether task or journey; nor put the work to task that hath been accustomed to journey.

None shall discover envy at the prosperity of a brother, nor supplant him, or put him out of his work, if he be capable to finish the same ; for no man can finish another's work so much to the lord's profit, unless he be thoroughly acquainted with the designs and draughts of him that begun it.

When a fellow Craftsman is chosen Warden of the work under the Master, he shall be true both to Master and fellows, shall carefully oversee the work in the Master's absence to the lord's profit ; and his brethren shall obey him.

All Masons employed shall meekly receive their wages without murmuring or mutiny, and not desert the master till the work is finished.

A younger brother shall be instructed in working, to prevent spoiling the materials for want of judgment, and for increasing and continuing of brotherly love.

All the tools in working shall be approved by the Grand Lodge.

No laborer shall be employed in the proper work of Masonry ; nor shall Freemasons work with those that are not free, without an urgent necessity ; nor shall they teach laborers and unaccepted Masons, as they should teach a brother or fellow.

VI. OF BEHAVIOR, viz :

I.   IN THE LODGE WHILE CONSTITUTED.

You are not to hold private committees, or separate conversation, without leave from the Master, nor to talk of anything impertinent or unseemly, nor interrupt the Master or Wardens, or any brother speaking to the Master ; nor behave yourself ludicrously or jestingly while the Lodge is engaged in what is serious and solemn ; nor use any unbecoming language upon any pretence whatsoever ; but to pay due reverence to your Master, Wardens, and Fellows, and put them to worship.

If any complaint be brought, the brother found guilty shall stand to the award and determination of the Lodge, who are the proper and competent judges of all such controversies (unless you carry it by appeal to the Grand Lodge,) and to whom they ought to be referred, unless a lord's work be hindered the meanwhile, in which case a particular reference may be made ; but you must never go to law about what concerns *Masonry*, without on absolute necessity apparent to the Lodge.

2.   BEHAVIOUR AFTER THE LODGE IS OVER AND THE BRETHREN NOT GONE.

You may enjoy yourself with innocent mirth, treating one another according to ability, but avoiding all excess, or forcing any brother to eat or drink beyond his inclination, or hindering him from going when his occasions call him, or doing or saying anything offensive, or that may forbid an *easy* and *free* conversation ; for that would blast our harmony and defeat our laudable purposes.

Therefore no private piques or quarrels must be brought within the door of the Lodge, far less quarrels about religion, or nations, or state policy, we being only as Masons of the catholic religion, above-mentioned; we are also of all nations, tongues, kindreds, and languages, and are resolved against *all politics*, as what never yet conduced to the welfare of the Lodge, nor ever will. This *Charge* has been always strictly enjoined and observed; but especially ever since the Reformation in Britain, or the dissent and secession of these nations from the communion of Rome.

3. BEHAVIOR WHEN BRETHREN MEET WITHOUT STRANGERS, BUT NOT IN A LODGE FORMED.

You are to salute one another in a courteous manner, as you will be instructed, calling each other *Brother*, freely giving mutual instruction as shall be thought expedient, without being overseen or overheard, and without encroaching upon each other, or derogating from that respect which is due to any brother, were he not a Mason; for though all Masons are as brethren upon the same level, yet Masonry takes no honor from a man that he had before; nay, rather it adds to his honor, especially if he has deserved well of the brotherhood, who must give honor to whom it is due, and avoid ill manners.

4. BEHAVIOR IN PRESENCE OF STRANGERS NOT MASONS.

You shall be cautious in your words and carriage, that the most penetrating stranger shall not be able to discover or find out what is not proper to be intimated; and sometimes you shall divert a discourse, and manage it prudently for the honor of the Worshipful Fraternity.

5. BEHAVIOR AT HOME AND IN YOUR NEIGHBORHOOD.

You are to act as becomes a moral and wise man; particularly, not to let your family, friends, and neighbors know the concerns of the Lodge, etc., but wisely to consult your own honor, and that of the Ancient Brotherhood, for reasons not to be mentioned here. You must also consult your health by not continuing together too late, or too long from home, after Lodge hours are past; and by avoiding of gluttony or drunkeness, that your families be not neglected or injured, nor you disabled from working.

6. BEHAVIOR TOWARD A STRANGER BROTHER.

You are cautiously to examine him, in such a method as prudence shall direct you, that you may not be imposed upon by an ignorant false pretender, whom you are to reject with contempt and derision, and beware of giving him any hints of knowledge.

But if you discover him to be a true and genuine brother, you are to respect him accordingly ; and if he is in want, you must re_lieve him if you can, or else direct him how he may be relieved ; you must employ him some days, or else recommend him to be employed. But you are not charged to do beyond your ability, only to prefer a poor brother, that is a good man and true, before any other poor people in the same circumstances.

Finally, All these CHARGES you are to observe, and also those that shall be communicated to you in another way ; cultivating brotherly love, the foundation and cap-stone, the cement and glory of this ancient fraternity, avoiding all wrangling and quarreling, all slander and backbiting, nor permitting others to slander any other brother, but defending his character, and doing him all good offices, as far as is consistent with your honor and safety and no further. And if any of them do you injury, you must apply to your own or his Lodge ; and from thence you may appeal to the Grand Lodge at the quarterly communication, and from thence to the annual Grand Lodge, as has been the ancient laudable conduct of our forefathers in every nation ; never taking a legal course, but when the case can not be otherwise decided, and patiently listening to the honest and friendly advice of Master and fellows when they would prevent you going to law with strangers, or would excite you to put a speedy period to all law-suits, that so you may mind the affair of Masonry with more alacrity and success ; but with respect to brothers or fellows at law, the Master and brethren should kindly offer their meditation, which ought to be thankfully submitted to by the contending brethren and if that submission is impracticable, they must, however, carry on their process or law-suit without wrath and rancor, (not in the common way,) saying or doing nothing which may hinder brotherly love, and good officers to be renewed and continued ; that all may see the benign influence of Masonry, as all true Masons have done from the beginning of the world, and will do to the end of time.

Amen. So mote it be.

THE

Twenty-Five Landmarks of Freemasonry.*

I.   The modes of recognition.

II.   The division of symbolic Masonry into three degrees.

III.   The legend of the third degree.

IV.   The government of the fraternity by a presiding officer called a *Grand Master*, who is elected from the body of the craft.

V.   The prerogative of the Grand Master to preside over every assembly of the craft, wheresover and whensoever held.

VI.   The prerogative of the Grand Master to grant dispensations for conferring degrees at irregular times.

VII.   The prerogative of the Grand Master to grant dispensations for opening and holding Lodges.

VIII.   The prerogative of the Grand Master to make Masons at sight.

IX.   The necessity for Masons to congregate in Lodges.

X.   The government of every Lodge by a Master and two Wardens.

XI.   The necessity, that every Lodge, when congregated, should be duly tiled.

XII.   The right of every Mason to be represented in all general meetings of the craft, and to instruct his representatives.

XIII.   The right of every Mason to appeal from the decision of his brethren in Lodge convened to the Grand Lodge or General Assembly of Masons.

XIV.   The right of every Mason to vist and sit in every regular Lodge.

XV.   That no visitor not known to some brother present as a Mason, can enter a Lodge without undergoing an examination.

XVI.   That no Lodge can interfere in the business or labor of another Lodge.

XVII.   That every Freemason is amendable to the laws and regulations of the Masonic jurisdiction in which he resides.

* A full explanation of and commentary on these Landmarks will be found in MACKEY'S "Text-Book of Masonic Jurisprudence," pp. 17-39.

XVIII.   That every candidate for initiation must be a man, free born and of lawful age.

XIX.   That every Mason must believe in the existence of God as the Grand Architect of the Universe.

XX.   That every Mason must believe in a resurrection to a future life.

XXI.   That a book of the law of God must constitute an indispensable part of the furniture of every Lodge.

XXII.   That all men in the sight of God are equal, and meet in the Lodge on one common level.

XXIII.   That Freemasonry is a secret society, in possession of secrets that can not be divulged.

XXIV.   That Freemasonry consists of a speculative science founded on an operative art.

XXV.   That the Landmarks of Masonry can never be changed.

These constitute the Landmarks, or, as they have sometimes been called "the body of Masonry," in which it is not in the power of any man, or body of men, to make the least innovation

CONSTITUTION

OF THE

M∴W∴GRAND LODGE

OF

Free and Accepted Masons

OF THE

STATE OF NEVADA, -

AS ADOPTED IN CONVENTION, JANUARY 17TH, A. L. 5865.

PART I.

Of the Organization of the Grand Lodge.

ARTICLE I.

OF ITS TITLE AND SEAL.

SECTION 1. This Grand Lodge shall be entitled "The Most Worshipful Grand Lodge of Free and Accepted Masons of the State of Nevada."

SEC. 2. It shall have a Seal, bearing such devices and inscriptions as may hereafter be determined; which shall be affixed to all instruments issued by or under its authority.

ARTICLE II.

OF ITS MEMBERS AND THEIR QUALIFICATIONS.

SECTION 1. The Grand Lodge shall be composed of a Grand Master, (whose address shall be *Most Worshipful*,) a Deputy Grand Master, a Senior Grand Warden, and a Junior Grand Warden, (whose addresses shall severally be *Right Worshipful*,) a Grand Treasurer and a Grand Secretary, (whose addresses shall severally be *Very Worshipful*,) and a Grand Chaplain, (whose address shall be *Very Reverend*,) a Grand Orator, a Grand Marshal, a Grand Standard Bearer, a Grand Sword Bearer, a Grand Bible Bearer, a Senior

Grand Deacon, a Junior Grand Deacon, two Grand Stewards, a Grand Organist, a Grand Pursuivant, and a Grand Tyler, (whose addresses shall severally be *Worshipful*,) and such other officers as it may hereafter designate ; together with all the Past Grand Officers and Past Masters of this jurisdiction, and the Masters and Wardens of the several chartered and duly constituted Lodges, or the representatives thereof, duly elected as provided in Art. II, Part VII.

SEC. 2. Each officer and member of the Grand Lodge must be a member of some Lodge within its jurisdiction. With the cessation of such membership, shall cease his office and membership in the Grand Lodge.

SEC. 3. No member of the Grand Lodge shall be represented therein by proxy.

ARTICLE III.

OF ITS POWERS AND AUTHORITY.

SECTION 1. The Grand Lodge is the Supreme Masonic Power and Authority in this State, possessing all the attributes of sovereignty and government—legislative, executive, and judicial—limited only by a strict adherence to the Ancient Landmarks of the Order, and to the provisions of its own Constitution and Regulations.

SEC. 2. Its legislative powers extend to every case of legislation, not expressly delegated by itself to the Lodges ; and the Constitutions and Regulations, which it has an inalienable right to adopt and promulgate at its own convenience, and to alter, amend, or repeal at its own pleasure, under the limitations therein imposed, are final and binding upon all Lodges and Masons within its jurisdiction, until so altered, amended, or repealed.

SEC. 3. Its executive powers include the granting of dispensations and charters to establish and perpetuate Lodges within this State, and in other territory where no Grand Lodge exists ; the revocation or suspension thereof; the issuing of special dispensations for all purposes permitted by any of the provisions of this Constitution ; and the exercise, generally, of all such authority as may be necessary to carry its own legislation into complete effect.

SEC. 4. Its judicial powers are of two kinds :—

1st. *Original*—Including the decision of all controversies between any of the Lodges, or between one of them and a member or members of another, or between members of different Lodges ; and the enforcement of discipline upon its own members and upon the Lodges under its jurisdiction : and

2d. *Appellate*—Embracing the revision of all matters of controversy or discipline, proper for Masonic investigation, which may have arisen in any of the Lodges, and over which it has not retained original jurisdiction.

ARTICLE IV.

OF ITS COMMUNICATIONS.

SECTION 1. The Grand Lodge shall hold its Annual Communications for the transaction of its regular business, at the City of Virginia, commencing on the second Tuesday of October, at 10 o'clock, A. M.

SEC. 2. Special Communications may be ordered by the Grand Master, whenever in his opinion, the welfare of the Fraternity shall require it.

SEC. 3. Special Communications shall be ordered by the Grand Master, upon an application therefor in writing, setting forth the causes which demand it, and signed by the Masters of at least three chartered Lodges.

SEC. 4. Every order for a Special Communication shall designate the object thereof so far as is proper to be written, and shall be issued to each Lodge and Grand Officer at least thirty days before the day named for meeting ; and no business shall be transacted thereat other than that for which the Grand Lodge was especially convened.

SEC. 5. The officers or representatives of at least five chartered Lodges shall be present in order to transact any business in the Grand Lodge, either at an Annual or Special Communication ; but upon occasions of ceremony only the Grand Master, or his duly authorized representative, with a sufficient number of brethren to fill the stations and places, may at any time open the Grand Lodge, and perform the ceremonies for which it was convened.

ARTICLE V.

OF ITS ELECTIONS AND APPOINTMENTS.

SECTION 1. The Grand Master, Deputy Grand Master, Grand Wardens, Grand Treasurer, and Grand Secretary shall be elected by ballot, at each Annual Communication, upon the fourth day thereof, unless the business of the Communication shall be sooner finished ; shall be installed before its close ; and shall hold their respective offices until their successors shall have been elected and installed. A majority of all the votes cast shall be necessary for an election.

SEC. 2. All other Grand Officers shall be appointed by the Grand Master, immediately after his installation, at each Annual Communication, and shall hold their respective offices during his will and pleasure.

SEC. 3. Whenever a vacancy shall occur in any elective office of the Grand Lodge, the Grand Master shall have power to fill the same by appointment which appointment shall be valid until the succeeding annual election and installation ; and the officer so appointed shall be charged with all the duties and responsibilities of one regularly elected.

ARTICLE VI.

Section 1. All questions in the Grand Lodge (except election of officers,) shall be decided either *viva voce*, or by a show of hands ; unless before the announcement of the result thereof, three members shall demand that the vote be taken by yeas and nays, in which case it shall thus be taken.

Sec. 2. Each Grand Officer present, whether elected or appointed, (except the Grand Tyler,) and each past Grand Officer present shall be entitled to one vote.

Sec. 3. Each Lodge represented shall be entitled to three votes and the Past Masters of each Lodge shall, collectively, be entitled to one vote.

Sec. 4. No Grand Officer, Past Grand Officer, or Past Master voting, or participating in a vote, in either of those capacities, shall vote, or participate in a vote, in any other of them ; but either of such members may, as Master, Warden, or representative of a Lodge, cast also the vote or votes to which such position shall entitle him.

Sec. 5. When a Lodge shall be represented by only two of its proper officers, the officer highest in rank may cast two of its three votes.

Sec. 6. When a Lodge shall be represented by only one of its proper officers, or by a representative, such officer or representative may cast all the votes to which it is entitled.

Sec. 7. In all cases of a tie vote, except votes by ballot, the Grand Master, in addition to his proper vote, may have the casting vote.

ARTICLE VII.

Section 1. The following regular committees, to consist of three members each, shall be appointed by the Grand Master at each Annual Communication, viz. : on Credentials, on Grievances, on Finances, on Jurisprudence, on Charters, on Returns, on By-Laws, and on Correspondence.

Sec. 2. Special committees may also be appointed by the Grand Master, whenever it may be deemed necessary by the Grand Lodge.

Sec. 3. No business of any kind shall be finally acted upon, until after reference to, and report upon by a committee, unless by unanimous consent ; and no appropriation of money shall be made until after reference to, and report upon by the committee on Finances.

ARTICLE VIII.

OF ITS REVENUES.

SECTION 1. The revenue of the Grand Lodge shall be derived from the following sources :—

1st. From fees charged for dispensations, charters, diplomas, and other documents issued under its authority.

2d. From contributions levied upon the Lodges, which shall always be equal and uniform, in proportion to their membership, admissions, and degrees conferred : and

3d. From the funds, dues, and proceeds of all property of dissolved Lodges within its jurisdiction.

SEC. 2. The following shall be the fees charged as above, exclusive of those provided in Sec. 3, Art. IV, Part II, to be paid to the Grand Secretary :—

1st. For a dispensation to form a new Lodge, the sum of one hundred dollars :

2d. ·For a charter to perpetuate a Lodge, the sum of seventy-five dollars :

3d. For a dispensation to hold an election of an officer or officers at a time other than that named in Sec. 1, Art. I, Part IV, the sum of ten dollars :

4th. For a dispensation to ballot for a candidate for the degrees, without the reference to a committee provided in Sec. 3, Art. III, Part III, the sum of ten dollars :

5th. For a dispensation to receive and act upon the petition of a rejected candidate, within a less period than twelve months prescribed in Sec. 2, Art. III, Part III, the sum of ten dollars : and

6th. For a diploma of any kind, the sum of two dollars, except when issued for the widow or children of a deceased Mason, in which case there shall be no charge; but no diploma shall issue except upon the presentation to the Grand Secretary of a certificate from the Secretary of a Lodge, in one of the forms prescribed in Art. III, Part VII.

SEC. 3. In no case shall either of the foregoing documents be issued until the fees therefor shall have been paid to the Grand Secretary.

SEC. 4. The following contributions shall be paid as annual dues, by each of the Lodges, whether chartered or under dispensation, at the time and in the manner provided in Sec. 4, Art. II, Part III :—

1st. For each degree it shall have conferred during the year, the sum of one dollar :

2d. For each member it shall have received by affiliation during the year, the sum of one dollar :

3d. For each Master Mason borne upon its roll at the date of its annual return, the sum of two dollars :

And the Grand Lodge may levy, in addition to the above, such other contributions as in its judgment may be required.

SEC. 5.   In case of the dissolution of a Lodge, the Grand Secretary, or some brother by him duly authorized, shall at once proceed to receive its funds on hand, collect its outstanding dues, and dispose of its jewels, furniture and property of every kind, in such manner as shall seem to him most judicious ; and he shall place the proceeds thereof, after the payment of necessary expenses, among the funds of the Grand Lodge.

PART II.

Of the Grand Officers, their Powers and Duties.

ARTICLE I.

OF THE GRAND MASTER.

SECTION 1. The Grand Master, during the interval between the Communications of the Grand Lodge, may exercise all of its executive powers as defined in Sec. 3, Art. III, Part I, except the granting of charters. By virtue of these, authority is given him—

1st. To grant dispensations for the formation of New Lodges, under the regulations prescribed in Sec. 2, Art. I, Part III :

2d. To grant dispensations for the holding elections of an officer or officers at times other than the regular periods prescribed in Sec. 1, Art. I. Part IV, under the regulations provided in Sec. 2, Art. I, Part IV :

3d. To grant dispensations to ballot for and confer the degrees upon candidates, without the reference of their applications to committees as provided in Sec. 3, Art. III, Part III, under the regulations prescribed in Sec. 4, Art. III, Part III :

4th. To grant dispensations to receive and act upon the petitions of rejected applicants, within a less period than the twelve months prescribed in. Sec. 2, Art. III, Part III, under the regulations provided in Sec. 4, Art. III, Part III :

5th. To convene any Lodge, preside therein, inspect its proceedings, and compel its conformity to Masonic usage :

6th. To arrest the charter or dispensation of any Lodge, for good reasons shown, and suspend the operations thereof until the next Annual Communication :

7th. To suspend the Master of any Lodge from the exercise of the powers and duties of his office, for good reasons shown, until the next Annual Communication :

8th. To require the attendance of, and information from any Grand Officer respecting matters appertaining to the duties of his office : and

9th. To appoint Representatives in other recognized Grand Lodges, and to receive and accredit such representatives from them.

SEC. 2. It shall be the duty of the Grand Master—

1st. To preside in the Grand Lodge at all its Communications:

2d. To present, at each Annual Communication, a written message, therein setting forth all his official acts during the year, exhibiting the general condition of Masonry within the jurisdiction, and recommending such legislation as he may deem necessary or expedient for the welfare of the Order:

3d. To constitute all chartered Lodges, either in person or by a duly authorized representative, in accordance with the ancient usages and regulations:

4th. To exercise a general and careful supervision over the Craft, and see that the Constitution and Regulations of the Grand Lodge are strictly maintained, supported, and obeyed: and

5th. To discharge all the necessary executive functions of the Grand Lodge, when that body is not in session.

ARTICLE II.

OF THE DEPUTY GRAND MASTER AND GRAND WARDENS.

SECTION 1. It shall be the duty of the Deputy Grand Master to assist the Grand Master in the discharge of his duties at all the Communications of the Grand Lodge, and, in his absence, to preside therein; and in the event of the death of the Grand Master, or his absence from the State, or of his inability from any cause to perform the functions of his office, the Deputy Grand Master shall succeed to and be charged with all his powers and duties.

SEC. 2. It shall be the duty of the Grand Wardens to assist the Grand Master at all the Communications of the Grand Lodge, and, in his absence, and that of the Deputy Grand Master to preside therein in the order of their rank; and, in case of the death, absence from the State, or inability as before, of both of their superiors, the Grand Wardens shall, in the order of their rank, succeed to and be charged with all the powers and duties of the Grand Master.

ARTICLE III.

OF THE GRAND TREASURER.

SECTION 1, It shall be the duty of the Grand Treasurer—

1st. To receive all moneys belonging to the Grand Lodge, from the Grand Secretary; to give him duplicate receipts therefor; and to keep, in proper books, a just account thereof:

2d. To take charge of all other property of the Grand Lodge, except as provided in Sec. I, Art. IV, of this Part, and keep an accurate account thereof:

3d.   To pay all orders drawn upon such funds and moneys, under such regulations as may be provided by the Grand Lodge:

4th.   To attend the Grand Lodge at all its Communications, and the Grand Master when required, with the books and all necessary papers appertaining to his office; and also, if required by the Grand Lodge or Grand Master, to attend with such books and papers upon any committee which may be appointed to act in relation to the fiscal concerns of the Grand Lodge: and

5th.   To report at each Annual Communication a detailed account of his receipts and disbursements, with proper vouchers for the latter; and to present a statement of the existing condition of its property and finances.

SEC. 2.   He shall execute and file in the office of the Grand Master, within fifteen days after his installation, an official bond, in such penal sum and with such sureties as shall be approved by the Grand Master, conditioned that he will faithfully discharge the duties of his office as prescribed in this Constitution, and, at the end of his term, pay over and transfer to his successor all funds or property of the Grand Lodge which shall have come into his keeping.

SEC. 3.   He shall receive such compensation for his services as the Grand Lodge may direct.

ARTICLE IV.

OF THE GRAND SECRETARY.

SECTION 1.   It shall be the duty of the Grand Secretary—

1st.   To record all the transactions of the Grand Lodge which it is proper to have written; and to superintend the publication thereof, immediately after the close of each Communication, under such instructions as may be given by the Grand Lodge:

2d.   To receive, duly file, and safely keep all papers and documents addressed or belonging to the Grand Lodge; and to present such as may require its action, at each Annual Communication thereof:

3d.   To keep the seal of the Grand Lodge, and affix the same with his attestation, to all instruments emanating from that body, and to all the written official acts of the Grand Master.

4th.   To collect all moneys due to the Grand Lodge, keep a correct account thereof in proper books, and pay the same quarterly to the Grand Treasurer:

5th.   To report, at each Annual Communication, a detailed account of all moneys received by him during the year, with a specific statement of the sources whence they were derived; and to present therewith the receipts of the Grand Treasurer therefor:

6th.   To report at each Annual Communication, all Lodges which shall be in arrears to the Grand Lodge, or which shall have neglected or refused to comply with any provision of its Constitution and Regulations:

7th. To conduct the correspondence of the Grand Lodge, and to submit copies thereof at each Annual Communication, for its inspection:

8th. To attend the Grand Lodge at all its Communications, and the Grand Master, when required, with the books and all necessary papers appertaining to his office:

9th. To keep his office, with all the books, papers, and archives of the Grand Lodge, in a fire-proof building; and to have the same open each day (except Sundays) for the transaction of Masonic business:

10th. To transmit to each Lodge within the jurisdiction, once in every three months, a list of all rejections, expulsions, suspensions, and restorations of which he shall have been notified by the several Lodges:

11th. To present, at each Annual Communication, an estimate of the probable expenses of the ensuing year, giving each class of expenditures under its proper head; and also to present an estimate of the probable income from the known sources of revenue, during the same period:

12th. To issue notices of any Special Communication ordered by the Grand Master to each Lodge and Grand Officer within this jurisdiction:

13th. To issue notices to each Lodge, of the granting of a dispensation by the Grand Master for the formation of a new Lodge.

14th. To transmit to any Lodge, which shall send him a certificate of membership and good standing of a deceased brother, in the form prescribed in Art. III, Part VII, stating that he leaves a wife, child, or children, a Grand Lodge Diploma for her, his or their benefit, free of charge, when so requested by such Lodge:

15th. To take charge of the jewels, furniture, clothing, and paraphernalia of the Grand Lodge, during its vacations:

16th. To furnish every Grand Officer, elected or appointed, with a certificate of such election or appointment:

17th. To act as Grand Librarian and take charge of the library of the Grand Lodge, under such regulations as it may prescribe:

18th. To report, at each Annual Communication, all unfinished business of the Grand Lodge; and to present all such other matters to its notice as may properly come within his province: and

19th. To perform all such other duties appertaining to his office, as the Grand Lodge may direct.

SEC. 2. He shall execute and file in the office of the Grand Master, within fifteen days after his installation, an official bond, in such penal sum, and with such sureties as shall be approved by the Grand Master, conditioned that he will faithfully discharge the duties of his office as prescribed in this Constitution.

SEC. 3.   He shall receive such compensation for his services as the Grand Lodge may direct; and in addition thereto shall receive the following fees ;

1st.   For a dispensation to open a new Lodge, the sum of Ten Dollars :

2d.   For a charter to perpetuate a Lodge, the sum of Ten Dollars :

3rd.   For a dispensation to hold an election of an officer or officers, at another than the regular period, the sum of Five Dollars.

4th.   For a dispensation to ballot for a candidate and confer the degrees, without reference to a committee, the sum of Five Dollars :

5th.   For a dispensation to receive and act upon the petition of a rejected applicant, within a less period than twelve months, the sum of Five Dollars :

6th.   For a diploma of any kind, (except when issued for the widow or children of a deceased brother,) the sum of Three Dollars : and

7th.   For every certificate (excep t those hereinbefore named) requiring the seal of the Grand Lodge, the sum of Three Dollars.

SEC. 4.   He may, with the approval of the Grand Master, appoint an Assistant Grand Secretary, for whose official acts he shall be responsible, and who shall be considered an appointed officer of the Grand Lodge, and shall receive such compensation for his services as it may direct.

ARTICLE V.

OF THE APPOINTED GRAND OFFICERS.

SECTION 1.   It shall be the duty of the Grand Chaplain, during each Communication of the Grand Lodge, to perform such services, appertaining to his office, as may be required of him by the Grand Master.

SEC. 2. It shall be the duty of the Grand Orator, at each Annual Communication, to deliver an address to the Grand Lodge upon matters appertaining to the Craft.

SEC. 3. It shall be the duty of the Grand Marshal—

1st.   To proclaim the Grand Officers at their installation, and to make such other proclamations as by the Grand Master may be directed :

2d.   To introduce the Representatives of other Grand Lodges, and all visiting brethren of distinction : and

3d. To conduct all processions of the Grand Lodge, under the direction of the Grand Master, and to perform such other duties, proper to his office, as may be required.

SEC. 4.   It shall be the duty of the Grand Standard Bearer to bear the Banner of the Grand Lodge in all processions and at all public ceremonies.

Sec. 5. It shall be the duty of the Grand Sword Bearer to attend upon the Grand Master, and bear the Sword of the Grand Lodge in all processions and at all public ceremonies.

Sec 6. It shall be the duty of the Grand Bible Bearer to bear the Holy Writings in all processions and at all public ceremonies.

Sec. 7. It shall be the duty of the Grand Deacons to assist the Grand Master and Grand Wardens in such manner as the ancient usages of the Craft prescribe.

Sec. 8. It shall be the duty of the Grand Stewards to superintend the preparations for all festive occasions directed by the Grand Lodge.

Sec. 9. It shall be the duty of the Grand Organist to preside at the organ at the opening and closing of the Grand Lodge, and to conduct its music upon all occasions of ceremony, when required.

Sec. 10. It shall be the duty of the Grand Pursuivant—

1st. To guard the inner door of the Grand Lodge, and communicate with the Grand Tyler without:

2d. To announce all applicants for admission by their names and proper Masonic titles, and see that all who enter wear the jewel and clothing proper to their rank: and

3d. To allow none to withdraw who have not obtained permission to do so from the Grand Master.

Sec. 11. It shall be the duty of the Grand Tyler—

1st. To guard the outer door of the Grand Lodge, and communicate with the Grand Pursuivant within:

2d. To report all applicants for admission to the Grand Pursuivant, and see that all who enter are duly authorized and properly clothed:

3d. To make suitable preparations for the accommodation of the Grand Lodge at all its Communications, and see that its hall is kept in proper condition during their continuance:

4th. To take charge of and safely keep the jewels, furniture, clothing, and paraphernalia of the Grand Lodge during its Communications: and

5th. To carry all notices and summonses, and perform such other duties as may be required of him by the Grand Lodge or Grand Master.

Sec. 12. The Grand Tyler shall receive for his services such compensation as the Grand Lodge may direct.

PART III.
Oj Subordinate Lodges.

ARTICLE I.
OF THE ORGANIZATION OF A LODGE.

Section 1. A Lodge can only be formed by authority of a

dispensation from the Grand Master, or of a charter from the Grand Lodge ; and no charter shall be granted to any Lodge until it shall have worked a time under dispensation, and shall have exhibited to the Grand Lodge satisfactory evidence of its Masonic capability.

SEC. 2.   Upon the petition of seven or more Master Masons being presented to the Grand Master, in the form prescribed in Art. III, Part VII, he may grant them a dispensation to open and hold a Lodge at the place therein to be named, with power to make Masons and receive members by affiliation ; and he shall therein appoint the Master and Wardens of the new Lodge.   But in no case shall such dispensation be issued, unless the petition be accompanied by a recommendation from the nearest or most convenient chartered Lodge, (if from a town or city where more than one Lodge exists, then from a majority of such lodges,) setting forth, in the form prescribed in Art. III, Part VII, that the petitioners are all Master Masons in good standing, that the establishment of the new Lodge is of manifest propriety and will conduce to the good of the Order, and that a safe and suitable Lodge room has been provided therefor ; nor unless the petition shall also be accompanied by a certificate of withdrawal of each petitioner from the Lodge of which he was last a member, and by a certificate from a Master, whom the Grand Master is satisfied is well skilled in the craft, declaring that the Master proposed in such petition is fully competent properly to confer the three degrees of Masonry, and to deliver entire the lectures thereunto appertaining.   Such dispensation shall terminate upon the first day of the month in which the next succeeding Annual Grand Communication shall be holden ; and shall then be returned to the Grand Secretary, together with the by-laws, book of records, and returns of the new Lodge to that date.

SEC. 3.   Upon the return of the dispensation of a new Lodge, as above, with a petition for a charter, in the form prescribed in Art. III, Part VII, if an examination of its work and proceedings shall prove satisfactory, the Grand Lodge may order the issue of a charter to such Lodge, and assign it such name and number on the registry as shall be deemed proper : and such Lodge shall be duly constituted within sixty days thereafter, or its charter shall be forfeited.   If the examination be not satisfactory, the petition may be totally refused, or a continuance of the dispensation, until the next Annual Grand Communication, may be ordered ; but no such continuance shall be granted a second time.

SEC. 4.   A Lodge shall consist of a Master, a Senior Warden, a Junior Warden, a Treasurer, a Secretary, a Senior Deacon, a Junior Deacon, a Tyler, and such other officers as its by-laws may provide ; together with as many members as it may find convenient.

ARTICLE II.

OF THE POWERS AND DUTIES OF A LODGE.

SECTION 1. The powers and duties of a Lodge are such as are prescribed in its dispensation or charter, by the Constitution and Regulations of the Grand Lodge, and by the general regulations of Masonry: and they are defined as follows:—

1st. *Executive*—In the direction and performance of its work, as prescribed by the Grand Lodge, under the control of the Master; and in all other matters, in aid of the Master, who is the primary executive authority of the Lodge:

2d. *Legislative*—Including all matters of legislation relative to its internal concerns, which shall not be in violation of the general regulations of Masonry, the Constitution or Regulations of the Grand Lodge, or its own particular by-laws: and

3d. *Judicial*—Embracing the exercise of discipline over its own members (except the Master) and all other Masons within its jurisdiction, and the settlement of controversies between them; subject always to a revision by the Grand Lodge, upon appeal.

SEC. 2. Each Lodge shall have not more than one stated Communication in each lunar month, but may hold such other communications as it may determine, or the Master shall direct ; but no business of any kind, except collections or appropriations for charity, conferring of degrees, ceremonial observances, election of Representatives to the communication of the Grand Lodge, or balloting for commissioners to try charges of unmasonic conduct, shall be done at any other than a stated communication, unless by dispensation from the Grand Master, as provided in Sec. 1, Art. I, Part II. And all business, except the examination of candidates and conferring of the subordinate degrees, shall be done in a Lodge of Master Masons.

SEC. 3. Each chartered and duly constituted Lodge shall be represented in the Grand Lodge at every communication, by one or more of its proper officers, or by a representative duly elected as provided in Art. II, Part VII, which representative shall have credentials in the form provided in Art. III. Part VII.

SEC. 4. Each chartered Lodge shall transmit to the Grand Secretary a full and correct return of its transactions for the twelve months next preceding the fifteenth day of August, in each year, within fifteen days thereafter, in the form provided in Art. III, Part VII ; and each Lodge under dispensation shall transmit a similar return from the date of its organization to the first day of October in each year, without delay ; and every Lodge shall accompany such return with payment of its dues to the Grand Lodge for those periods, as prescribed in Sec. 4, Art. VIII, Part I.

SEC. 5. Each Lodge shall transmit to the Grand Secretary a copy of its by-laws, as soon as adopted : but no such by-laws, nor any subsequent amendment thereunto, shall be deemed valid until approved by the Grand Lodge, though they may be acted under until the next Annual Communication, if approved by the Grand Master.

SEC. 6. Each chartered Lodge shall, within two months from the date of its charter, provide a suitable seal, bearing such devices as may be deemed proper, and having inscribed thereon the name and number of the Lodge, and the place of its location ; and all documents or papers of every kind whatsoever, emanating from such Lodge, or from its Master or Secretary, in his official capacity, shall bear the impress of such seal, or be considered null and of no effect.

SEC. 7. Each Lodge shall have all official communications from the Grand Master or Grand Secretary read in open Lodge at the stated communication next following their receipt.

SEC. 8. Each Lodge shall provide the several books prescribed in Sec. 2, Art. V, Part IV, to be kept by its Secretary, which shall be prepared in accordance with forms to be provided.

SEC. 9. Each Lodge may provide, in such manner as it may deem proper, for the payment of its officers or representatives in attending the communications of the Grand Lodge.

SEC. 10. For the neglect or violation of any duty imposed upon a Lodge in this Constitution, its charter may be suspended or forfeited: and for the neglect or violation of any duty herein imposed upon a Secretary, his Lodge shall be held responsible.

ARTICLE III.

OF PROHIBITIONS.

SECTION 1. No Lodge shall remove its place of meeting from that named in its dispensation or charter, unless notice shall have been given at a stated communication that a resolution for such removal will be offered at the next succeeding one, nor unless such resolution shall have been adopted by the votes of at least two-thirds of the members present at such succeeding communication ; nor shall such removal then take place until the action of the Lodge shall have been approved by the Grand Lodge or Grand Master.

SEC. 2. No Lodge in this State shall receive an application for the degrees of Masonry unless the applicant shall have been a resident within the State during twelve months, and within the jurisdiction of the Lodge during six months, next preceding the date of his application. Nor shall any Lodge receive such application from any person, who, within twelve months next preceding, shall have been rejected by any Lodge, unless by dispensation from the Grand Master, as provided in Sec. 1, Art. I, Part II. All such applications, as well as those for affiliation, shall be in writing, signed by the applicant, and recommended by at least two members of the Lodge, in the forms prescribed in Art. III, Part VII.

Sec. 3. No Lodge shall ballot upon such application, (except by dispensation from the Grand Master, as provided in Sec. 1, Art. I, Part II,) until it shall have been referred to a committee, whose duty it shall be to make strict examination into the moral, mental, and physical qualifications of the applicant, and to report thereon at the next stated meeting, unless further time be granted. No application shall be withdrawn after reference to a committee, and it shall require an unanimous ballot to elect. But if one black ball, only, appear in the ballot box, the Master without declaring the result, may at once order a second ballot for the purpose of correcting a possible mistake.

Sec. 4. No dispensation shall be issued to a Lodge to ballot for and confer the degrees upon a candidate without reference to a committee, as provided in the preceding section, nor to receive and act upon the petition of a rejected applicant within less than twelve months after the date of such rejection, unless the application therefor be made by the Lodge, by a unanimous vote ; and of the special communication to be holden under such dispensation, and the purpose thereof, the members of the Lodge shall have due notice.

Sec. 5. No Lodge, unless it be otherwise provided in its by-laws, shall have more than one ballot for the three degrees ; but, though an applicant may be elected to receive them, if, at any time before his initiation, objection be made by any member, he shall not receive the degree until such objection shall have been withdrawn ; and if, after his initiation, but before being passed, or after passing, before being raised, objection to his advancement be made by any member, such objection shall be referred to a committee, with power to inquire into the cause thereof, who shall at the next stated communication, (unless further time be given,) report thereon ; and upon the reception of such report, if no cause for the objection has been assigned, or if the cause assigned be, in the opinion of two-thirds of the members present, not a valid and Masonic one, the Lodge may confer the degree in the same manner as if no objection had been made.

Sec. 6. No Lodge shall advance an Entered Apprentice or a Fellow Craft to a higher degree until, after a strict examination in open Lodge, he shall have given satisfactory evidence that he is entirely proficient and well qualified in that or those which he has already taken ; and no Entered Apprentice or Fellow Craft shall be advanced to a higher degree in any Lodge other than that in which he shall have received those, or either of those degrees, unless by the official consent of such Lodge, if it then be in existence.

Sec. 7. No Lodge within this State shall confer the three degrees for a less fee than fifty dollars ; nor shall any Lodge without the State, and under this jurisdiction, confer them for a less fee than thirty dollars ; and in every case the fee for each or all of the degrees, as may be regulated by the Lodge, shall accompany the application.

SEC. 8. No Lodge shall confer degrees upon more than five candidates at any one communication ; nor shall confer more than one degree upon any one candidate at any communication ; nor shall confer either of the degrees upon more than one candidate at a time.

SEC. 9. No Lodge shall expel a member for the non-payment of his dues ; but in case any member shall have refused or neglected to pay his regular dues during a period of six months, he shall be notified by the Secretary that, unless at the next stated communication, either his dues be paid, or sickness or inability to pay be shown as the cause of such refusal or neglect, he will be suspended from all the rights and privileges of Masonry. If neither of these things be done, he shall be so suspended, unless for special reasons shown, the Lodge may otherwise determine; but any Mason thus suspended, who shall at any time pay the arrearages due at the time of his suspension, together with such further dues as would, had he retained his membership, have accrued against him to the date of such payment, shall by that act be restored.

SEC. 10. No Lodge shall receive lectures from any person who is not duly authorized by the Grand Lodge or the Grand Master.

SEC. 11. No Lodge shall receive an application for affiliation unless it be accompanied by a proper dimit from the Lodge of which the applicant was last a member, or a satisfactory explanation, in writing, of his inability to furnish such dimit.

SEC. 12. No Lodge shall hold Masonic communication with any Lodge which has been declared illegal by the Grand Lodge, or with any person who has received degrees in, or is a member of such a Lodge.

SEC. 13. No Lodge shall admit a visitor without due inquiry or examination, nor if there be, in the opinion of the Master, a valid objection made to such admission by a member of the Lodge.

SEC. 14. No Lodge which shall have failed to make its annual returns, as provided in Sec. 4, Art. II, Part III, and in Sec. 1, Art. V, Part IV. shall be entitled to representation at the next Grand Communication.

SEC. 15. No Lodge, until chartered and duly constituted, shall be entitled to representation in the Grand Lodge ; but a Lodge under dispensation may send delegates thereto, who may be admitted to seats and be permitted to speak, but shall have no vote.

ARTICLE IV.

OF THE DISSOLUTION OF LODGES.

SECTION 1. A Lodge may be dissolved—

1st. By the voluntary surrender of its charter, when such surrender shall have been accepted by the Grand Lodge: and

2d. By the revocation of its charter by the Grand Lodge.

Sec. 2. The charter of a Lodge may be surrendered if notice shall be given at a stated communication that a resolution to that effect will be presented at the next succeeding one, and if, at such succeeding communication, there shall not be seven members present who oppose such resolution ; but no such act of surrender shall be considered final until it shall have been approved and accepted by the Grand Lodge.

Sec. 3. The charter of a Lodge may be forfeited—

1st. By disobedience of any provision of the constitution or Regulations of the Grand Lodge :

2d. By disregard of the lawful authority of the Grand Master :

3d. By violation or neglect of the ancient and recognized usages of the Craft : or

4th. By failure to meet during a period of six successive months. But no charter shall be forfeited unless charges against the Lodge shall have been presented to and investigated in the Grand Lodge, of which charges the Lodge accused shall have had due notice ; though the same may be arrested until the next Annual Grand Communication either by the Grand Lodge or the Grand Master, upon satisfactory reasons therefor being shown.

Sec. 4. The forfeiture or arrest of the charter of a Lodge involves the suspension of all its members from the rights and privileges of Masonry, excepting those who may be specially exempted from such effect.

Sec. 5. The surrender or forfeiture of the charter of a Lodge, when declared by the Grand Lodge, shall be conclusive upon the Lodge and its members ; and all its funds, jewels, furniture, dues, and property of every kind shall be disposed of, as provided in Sec. 5, Art. VIII, Part I.

PART IV.

Of the Officers of Subordinate Lodges.

ARTICLE I.

OF ELECTIONS AND APPOINTMENTS.

Section 1. The Master, Wardens, Treasurer, and Secretary of each Lodge shall be elected annually, by ballot, at the stated communication next preceding the anniversary of St. John the Evangelist; and a majority of the votes of the members present shall be necesrary to elect. They shall be installed as soon as practicable thereafter, and shall hold their respective offices until their successors shall have been duly elected and installed.

Sec. 2. In case any Lodge shall fail to hold such election at the time above named, upon good cause being shown therefor, the Grand Master may issue a dispensation to hold such election at another time; and in case a vacancy shall at any time occur in either of the offices of Master or Warden in any Lodge, upon proper representation of the necessity therefor, the Grand Master may issue a dispensation for an election to fill such vacancy. But in either of these cases, such dispensation shall be issued only upon the application of the Lodge, setting forth the reasons therefor, to be approved by two-thirds of the members present at a stated communication, and to be properly certified by the Secretary ; and of the special election which may thus be ordered, the members shall have due notice.

Sec. 3. Every member in good standing, and whose dues are paid, shall be entitled to a vote at all elections ; and every voter shall be eligible to any office in the Lodge.

Sec. 4. The Deacons, Tyler, and such other subordinate officers as the by-laws of each Lodge may designate, shall be appointed in such manner as they may direct : and the officers so appointed shall be properly invested as soon as practicable after their appointment.

ARTICLE II.

OF THE MASTER.

Section 1. The Master shall have power—

1st. To congregate his Lodge whenever he shall deem it proper :

2d. To issue or casue to be issued, all summonses and notices which may be required :

3d. To discharge all the executive functions of his Lodge: and

4th. To perform all such other acts, by ancient usage proper to his office, as shall not be in contravention of any provision of the Constitution or Regulations of the Grand Lodge.

Sec. 2. It shall be his duty—

1st. To preside at all communications of his Lodge :

2d. To confer all degrees in strict accordance with the ritual which may hereafter be ordained by the Grand Lodge:

3d. To give, in full, the lectures appertaining to each degree, at the time it is conferred, in accordance with such ritual :

4th. To superintend the official acts of all the officers of his Lodge, and see that their respective duties are properly discharged : and

5th. To carefully guard against any infraction, by the members of his Lodge, of its own by-laws, of the Constitution or Regulations of the Grand Lodge, or of the general regulations of Masonry.

Sec. 3. From the decisions of the Master there shall be no appeal to the Lodge ; but objections to such decisions may be laid before the Grand Master, and by him be dealt with in the manner provided in Art. II, Part VI.

Sec. 4. In all cases of a tie vote, except votes by ballot, the Master, in addition to his proper vote, may have the casting vote.

Sec. 5. For the neglect or violation of any duty imposed by this Constitution upon the Master of a Lodge, he shall be subject to deprivation of office, suspension or expulsion, as provided in Art. II, Part VI.

ARTICLE III.

OF THE WARDENS.

Section 1. It shall be the duty of the Wardens to assist the Master in the performance of his duties, and to discharge all those duties which ancient usage has assigned to their respective stations.

Sec. 2. In the absence of the Master, the Senior Warden, (and in his absence also, the Junior Warden,) shall succeed to and be charged with all the powers and duties of the Master.

ARTICLE IV.

OF THE TREASURER.

Section 1. It shall be the duty of the Treasurer—

1st. To receive and safely keep all moneys or property of every kind which shall be placed in his hands by order of the Lodge:

2d. To disburse or transfer the same, or any part thereof, upon the order of the Master, duly attested by the Secretary :

3d. To keep a book or books wherein a correct account of his receipts and disbursements shall be exhibited :

4th. To present a statement of the finances of the Lodge whenever required : and

5th. To perform such other duties, appertaining to his office, as the by-laws may require, or the Lodge may at any time direct.

ARTICLE V.

OF THE SECRETARY.

Section 1. It shall be the duty of the Secretary—

1st. To record all the proceedings at each communication, which it is proper should be written, under the direction of the Master ; and to submit such record to the Lodge at its next stated communication for approval or correction:

2d. To prepare and transmit a copy of such record, or of any part thereof, to the Grand Lodge, when required :

3d. To collect and receive all moneys due to the Lodge, and pay them over to the Treasurer :

4th. To keep the seal of the Lodge, and to affix the same, with his attestation, to all papers issued under its authority, or in obedience to the requirements of the Constitution and Regulations of the Grand Lodge:

5th. To transmit to the Grand Secretary, immediately after each election and installation in the Lodge, a certificate thereof, in the form prescribed in Art. III, Part VII:

6th. To transmit to the Grand Secretary the annual return required in Sec. 4, Art. II, Part III, in the form provided in Art. III, Part VII: and

7th. To report to the Grand Secretary, immediately after their occurrence, all rejections, expulsions, suspensions, and restorations, in the forms provided in Art. III, Part VII.

SEC. 2   He shall keep the following books of the Lodge, in such forms as may be provided:—

1st. A Record Book, in which he shall record all the transactions of the Lodge, proper to be written, after the same shall have been approved:

2d. A Book of By-Laws, for the signatures of the members in the order of their admission:

3d. A Roll Book, in which he shall record, upon pages alphabetically arranged, the names of all belonging to the Lodge ; the dates of their initiation, passing, raising, or affiliation ; the name, number, and location of the Lodges of which those affiliated were last members: the age and occupation of each when received ; and the dates of their withdrawal, expulsion, suspension, death, or restoration:

4th. A Black Book, in which he shall record, upon pages alphabetically arranged, the names of those rejected, expelled, suspended, or restored by any of the Lodges, so far as he shall receive the proper notice thereof: and

5th. A Register to be kept in the Tyler's room, in which all members shall record their names, and all. visitors shall record their names, and the names, numbers, and locations of their respective Lodges, before entering the Lodge.

SEC. 3. He shall also keep such Account Books as may be necessary to present clearly the account of each member with the Lodge, the receipts of the Secretary, and his payments to the Treasurer ; and shall preserve the Books of Constitutions and Regulations of the Grand Lodge, which may from time to time be published, together with all the printed proceedings thereof, as promulgated by its order.

ARTICLE VI.

OF THE APPOINTED OFFICERS.

SECTION 1. The Deacons, Tyler, and other appointed officers, shall perform such duties consonant with the usages of the Craft and appertaining to their respective offices, as may be required by the by-laws, or directed by the Master.

PART V.
Of Individual Masons.

ARTICLE I.

OF MEMBERSHIP.

SECTION. 1. Membership in a Lodge may be acquired—
1st. By having regularly received the degree of Master Mason therein:
2d. By having been duly elected for affiliation therewith: and
3d. By having been named in a dispensation for a new Lodge as one of the petitioners therefor.

SEC. 2. No Mason shall be a member of more than one Lodge at the same time.

SEC. 3. Membership in a Lodge can only be terminated—
1st. By the dissolution of the Lodge:
2d. By voluntary withdrawal therefrom: and
3d. By death, suspension, or expulsion.

SEC. 4. A member of a Lodge, in good standing, and whose dues are paid, may withdraw therefrom at any time by giving notice of his intention so to do at a stated communication; but no recommendatory certificate shall be given him, except by a vote of a majority of the members of the Lodge then present.

ARTICLE II.

OF DUTIES, PROHIBITIONS, AND PENALTIES.

SECTION 1. It is the duty of every Master Mason to be a Member of some Lodge; and every one who, having resided six months within the jurisdiction of a Lodge, shall refuse or neglect to make application so to be, or who shall not have regularly contributed to such Lodge an amount equivalent to its regular dues, while able so to do, shall be deemed unworthy of Masonic consideration, and shall not be entitled to, nor be the recipient of, any of the rights, privileges, or charities of the Order.

SEC. 2. No member of a Lodge shall be required to divulge his vote upon a ballot for affiliation, or for the degrees of Masonry; nor assign reasons for such vote, if it be known.

SEC. 3. No Mason shall hold any Masonic intercourse with an

expelled or suspended Mason, with an illegal Lodge, with any person who has received degrees therein, or is a member thereof, nor with any Mason not acknowledged as such by this Grand Lodge.

SEC. 4. For non-payment of his dues, a member may be suspended from all the rights and privileges of Masonry, in the manner provided in Sec. 9, Art. III, Part III.

SEC. 5. For any violation of the Ancient Landmarks of the Order, of the Constitution or Regulations of the Grand Lodge, of the by-laws of his Lodge, or of any portion of the Masonic or moral law, a member, or any other Mason within the jurisdiction of a Lodge, may be reprimanded, suspended, or expelled, in the manner provided in Art. III, Part VI.

PART VI.

Of Trials, Appeals, and Penalties.

ARTICLE I.

RELATIVE TO MASTERS OF LODGES.

SECTION 1. Charges may be preferred against the Master of a Lodge for abuse of his power, violation of the Constitution or Regulations, or for unmasonic conduct of any kind, by any five Master Masons in good standing ; which charges shall be in writing, over their signatures, and shall be presented to the Grand Lodge, if in session, or to the Grand Master during the vacation.

SEC. 2. Upon the presentation of such charges, the Grand Lodge, or the Grand Master, as the case may be, may at once appoint and summon not less than three nor more than seven disinterested Masters, to assemble as Commissioners to hear and determine thereupon ; and shall then summon the accused to appear and answer thereunto, at such time and place most convenient for the parties as shall be indicated in said summons ; giving him, if within the jurisdiction of his Lodge, at least ten days—if without that jurisdiction and within the State, at least thirty days—and if without the State, at least ninety days—to answer thereunto; and transmitting to him also a copy of the charges.

SEC. 3. The Commissioners, thus assembled, shall choose one of their number to preside, and they, or any of them, shall have power to summon witnesses at the request of either party. The witnesses, if Masons, shall testify upon their honor as such ; if not, their depositions shall be taken, in writing, before an officer legally authorized to administer oaths ; and, in such case, the party requiring such depositions shall notify the other of the time and place when and where they will be taken, that he may, if he choose, be present thereat.

SEC. 4. The Commissioners may adjourn from time to time, at their own convenience, or for good cause shown by either party; provided that the period within which their duties shall be concluded, shall not exceed ten days, unless, for sufficient reasons, the Grand Master shall grant them further time.

SEC. 5. The opinion of a majority of the Commissioners shall be deemed the judgment of the whole, and shall be conclusive, unless an appeal be taken at the next Annual Communication of the Grand Lodge.

SEC. 6. The penalties which may be inflicted by such Commissioners, may be either deprivation of office, suspension, or expulsion, as in their judgment shall seem proper.

SEC. 7. The Commissioners shall keep a complete record of their proceedings and of their judgment, and shall transmit the same to the Grand Secretary, at the conclusion of the trial; and the judgment shall at once be carried into effect by order of the Grand Master.

SEC. 8. An Appeal to the Grand Lodge may be taken at its next Annual Grand Communication, by either party, if notice thereof be given to the Grand Secretary within thirty days after the conclusion of the trial.

ARTICLE II.

RELATIVE TO LODGES AND MEMBERS OF DIFFERENT LODGES.

SECTION 1. When a controversy shall arise between Lodges, or between a Lodge and a member or members of another Lodge, charges may be preferred by either party, if in good standing; which charges shall be in writing, and shall be presented to the Grand Lodge or Grand Master, as provided in Sec. 1, Art. I, of this Part.

SEC. 2. Upon the presentation of such charges, not less than five nor more than seven Commissioners shall be appointed and summoned, as provided in Sec. 2, Art, I, of this Part, which Commissioners shall be Masters or Wardens, and shall be selected from at least three different Lodges not interested in the controversy, and most convenient to the parties; and the accused party shall be summoned, with such time to answer as provided in the section and article last quoted.

SEC. 3. The Commissioners shall have power to proceed, and shall keep a record of their proceedings and judgment in the same manner as provided in Art. I, of this Part; and the penalties which they may inflict may be any known to Masonic usage, or, if the case be one not involving a violation of Masonic duty, the decision may be such special one as the circumstances shall, in their judgment warrant.

Sec. 4.   An appeal may be taken by either party to the Grand Lodge, as provided in Sec. 8, Art. I, of this Part.

ARTICLE III.

RELATIVE TO MASONS INDIVIDUALLY.

SECTION 1.   When any member of a Lodge, (except its Master or the Grand Master,) or any Mason residing within its jurisdiction, shall be accused of unmasonic conduct, charges to that effect may be preferred by any Master Mason in good standing; which charges shall be in writing, over his signature, and shall be presented to the Master of the Lodge having jurisdiction thereof.

Sec. 2.   Upon the presentation of such charges, it shall be the duty of the Master, by due notification, to call a special communication of his Lodge, as soon as practicable, and there cause to be elected, by ballot, and by a majority of those present, not less than seven nor more than nine of its members, who shall assemble as Commissioners, to hear and determine thereupon, at such time and place, convenient to the parties, as he shall indicate; and he shall also summon the accused to appear and answer thereunto at such time and place; and shall, at the same time, cause the Secretary to furnish him with a copy of the charges, and to notify the accuser of the said time and place of trial.   .

Sec. 3.   If the accused be within the jurisdiction of the Lodge, the summons and copy of the charges shall be issued at least ten days prior to the day appointed for the trial, and shall be served personally by the Tyler, or shall be left at his ordinary residence or place of business.   If he be without the said jurisdiction, but within the State, and his residence be known, they shall be issued at least thirty days before the day of trial, and shall be forwarded to his address by the Secretary, by mail or other usual mode of conveyance, which shall be deemed sufficient service.   If he be without the State, and his residence be known, they shall be issued at least ninety days before the trial, and shall be forwarded to his address by the Secretary, as before provided, which shall be sufficient service.   If his address is unknown, the Master shall allow the trial to proceed at once upon the testimony, ex parte.

Sec. 4.   The Commissioners shall assemble at the time and place appointed, and shall be presided over by the Master of the Lodge, who shall decide all questions of Masonic law, which may arise during the trial, but shall not have a vote in the final decision of the case by the Commissioners ; and the Secretary, by order of the Master, shall attend them to keep a full and correct record of the proceedings, testimony, and of the judgment, under their supervision.

Sec. 5.   The Master shall summon such witnesses, within the jurisdiction of his Lodge, as may be desired by either party, and the accused may select any brother in good standing to assist him in his defence. The witnesses, if Masons, shall testify on their honor as such : if not, their depositions shall be taken in writing, before an officer legally authorized to administer oaths, and in such case, the party requiring such depositions shall notify the other of the time and place when and where they will be taken, that he may, if he choose, be present thereat.

SEC. 6. The Commissioners may adjourn from time to time, at their own convenience, or for sufficient cause shown by either party ; provided that the period within which their duties shall be concluded shall not exceed ten days, unless for good reasons shown, the Master shall grant them further time.

SEC. 7. After all the testimony shall have been received, the Commissioners shall proceed to deliberate upon their verdict and sentence, with none present save themselves and the Secretary, which last shall have no voice in the proceedings. The judgment of a majority of the Commissioners shall be taken as the decision of the whole ; and when the trial is concluded, the Secretary shall make a fair copy of the record and finding, under their supervision, which shall be signed by the chairman of such Commission, and attested by the Secretary, and shall be presented to the Master, who, at the next communication of his Lodge, shall, in the presence of its members only, announce the result, and direct the Secretary to record the same as the judgment of the Lodge, and file the record for safe keeping among its archives.

SEC. 8. The penalties which may be inflicted are reprimand in open Lodge, suspension, or expulsion. If the sentence be reprimand, the Master shall summon the adjudged to appear at the next stated communication, when it shall be carried into effect, in the presence only of members of the Lodge. If it be suspension or expulsion, it shall at once go into effect, and the Secretary shall immediately notify the Grand Secretary thereof; and it shall be final and conclusive, unless an appeal be taken to the Grand Lodge.

SEC. 9. An appeal may be taken to the Grand Lodge by either party, at its next succeeding Annual Communication, but not unless a notice of such intended appeal shall be given to the Master within thirty days after his announcement of the result of the trial ; and in all cases of expulsion or suspension, the Master shall cause the Secretary to prepare a transcript of the record of trial, and immediately transmit it to the Grand Secretary, together with information of the appeal intended, if any there be.

ARTICLE IV.

OF REVISIONS AND RESTORATIONS.

SECTION 1. All judgments from which an appeal shall be taken as hereinbefore in this Part provided, shall be reviewed in the Grand Lodge, or before a committee thereof, during its communications, upon the record sent up, and upon such other proper documents as may be submitted ; and its decision shall be final and conclusive.

SEC. 2.   All sentences of suspension shall be for an indefinite period ; and a Lodge may at any stated communication, by the votes of two-thirds of the members present, annul any such sentence of suspension pronounced by itself, and restore the Mason thus suspended to all his Masonic rights ; provided, that notice of a resolution for such restoration shall have been given at the stated communication next preceding.   And in case of such restoration, the Secretary shall at once notify the Grand Secretary thereof.

SEC. 3.   The Grand Lodge may, at any Annual Grand Communication, if good cause therefor be shown, restore a Mason who has been suspended or expelled within its jurisdiction; but such restoration shall not restore him to membership in the Lodge by which he was suspended or expelled.

SEC. 4.   No suspension, expulsion, or restoration shall be published otherwise than as hereinbefore provided, except by authority of the Grand Lodge, or by order of the Grand Master.

SEC. 5.   When it is the intention of any Lodge to take measures to apply to the Grand Lodge for the restoration of a Mason who has been expelled, it shall be the duty of the Master thereof to notify the members of his Lodge, as far as possible, of the time when such proposed action will be had ; and cause to be spread upon the minutes of the communication at which such action shall be had, the fact that such notification was duly given.

PART VII.

Of Amendments, Definitions, and Forms.

ARTICLE I.

OF AMENDMENTS.

SECTION 1. Any proposed amendment to this Constitution shall be presented at an Annual Grand Communication, and shall in all cases be referred to the Committee on Jurisprudence, who shall report before a vote thereon be taken.

SEC. 2. After the report of said committee, if the vote in favor of such proposed amendment be unanimous, it shall be declared adopted ; and from and after the close of that communication, shall become a part of the Constitution.

SEC. 3. If the vote in favor of such proposed amendment be not unanimous, but there be a majority therefor, it shall lie over for one year, and shall be published with the proceedings, under the caption of "Proposed Amendments to the Constitution ;" and if, at the next succeeding Annual Grand Communication, it shall receive two-thirds of the votes given therein, it shall be declared adopted, and from and after the close of that Communication, shall become a part of the Constitution.

SEC. 4. No vote upon a proposed amendment shall be taken after the election of. the Grand Officers.

ARTICLE II.

OF DEFINITIONS.

The words and terms used in this Constitution shall bear the construction which is given them in the following definitions :—

GRAND MASTER.—This title applies, not only to him who has been elected and installed as Grand Master, but to either of the Grand Officers who, under the provisions of Art. II, Part II, of this Constitution, shall have succeeded to the powers and duties of the Grand Master.

MASTER.—This title applies, not only to him who has been elected and installed as Master, but to either of the Wardens, who under the provisions of Art. III, Part IV, of this Constitution, shall have succeeded to the powers and duties of the Master.

PAST GRAND OFFICER.—This title applies only to one of the six elective Grand Officers who has been regularly elected and installed, and has served his term as such in this Grand Lodge ; and who remains a member, in good standing, of some Lodge under its jurisdiction.

PAST MASTER.—This title applies only to one who has been regularly elected, or named in a charter, and installed, and has served a term as Master of a chartered Lodge; and who is a member, in good standing, of a subordinate Lodge of this jurisdiction.

REPRESENTATIVE.—The representative of a Lodge within this State, is one who, being a member thereof, in the event that neither the Master nor either of the Wardens can be present at the Grand Lodge, has been elected by the Lodge, at a stated communication, or at a special communication called for that purpose, by ballot, and by a majority of the votes present to represent it at the next Grand Communication. A Lodge without the State, may be represented by a member of any Lodge under this jurisdiction, elected as before.

VACANCY.—Vacancies in office, either in a Lodge or in the Grand Lodge, may occur by death, deprivation, removal from the jurisdiction, suspension or expulsion.

JURISDICTION.—The jurisdiction of the Grand Lodge includes all Lodges and Masons within the Territorial limits of this State, and all Lodges and their members without this State, acting under its authority.

The jurisdiction of a Lodge includes all Masons residing nearer to its place of meeting than to that of any other Lodge within this State, except in towns or cities where more than one Lodge exists; in which case, each of such Lodges has separate jurisdiction over its own members, and concurrent jurisdiction over all Masons not members of one of such Lodges, who reside in such town or city, or nearer thereto than to any other place where a Lodge exists.

REGULATION.—By a regulation of the Grand Lodge is meant any resolution, edict, law, or ordinance of any kind whatever, other than the Constitution, which it may adopt.

SUSPENSION.—The suspension of a Lodge is an arrest of its charter, and a temporary prohibition to assemble or work as a legal Lodge, until again authorized so to do by competent authority; and the act suspends all its members except those especially exempted from its effect.

The suspension of the Master of a Lodge is a temporary deprivation of his office and prohibits all recognition of him in that capacity, until he be restored by competent authority.

The suspension of a Mason is a temporary deprivation of all his rights and privileges as such, and prohibits all Masons and Lodges from holding any Masonic intercourse whatever with him, until he shall be legally restored by the Lodge which suspended him, or by the Grand Lodge.

EXPULSION.—The expulsion of a Mason is the highest penalty known to the Masonic law. It is an absolute deprivation of all the rights and privileges of the Order, and prohibits all Masons and Lodges from holding any Masonic intercourse with him forever, unless he be restored by the Grand Lodge.

NOTIFICATION.—A notification is a call issued by the Secretary, by order of the Lodge or Master, or by other competent authority as hereinbefore provided, to attend for some specific purpose at the time and place therein indicated; and it is the duty of every Mason to comply with its direction, if he can, without great inconvenience, do so.

SUMMONS.—A summons is an imperative order, issued by the Master, or by other competent authority as hereinbefore provided, to appear at such time and place as may therein be designated. The obligation to obey it is absolute, and the penalty for disobedience shall be expulsion, unless it shall be shown that such disobedience was unavoidable, or was occasioned by some pressing necessity.

STATED COMMUNICATIONS. — The stated communication of a Lodge is the one only communication in each lunar month, at which busines may be done, with the exceptions specified in Sec. 2, Art. II, Part III. It shall be designated as such in the by-laws of each Lodge, and no adjourned or called communication shall ever be considered as a part of such stated communication.

ARTICLE III.

OF FORMS.

FORM *of Certificate for a Diploma.*

...............Lodge, No......., F. and A. M., }
.....................................A. L. 58... }

To the Very Worshipful..,

Grand Secretary of the Grand Lodge of Nevada:—

I hereby certify that Brother.................is a Master Mason and a member of this Lodge, in good standing ; and as such he is hereby recommended for a Grand Lodge Diploma, upon payment of the usual fees.

Given under my hand and the Seal of the Lodge afore-
[Seal.]   said, at the date above written.

...............:...*Secretary.*

FORM *of Certificate for a Diploma for the benefit of the family of a deceased Brother.*

...............Lodge, No......., F. and A. M., }
.....................................A. L. 58... }

To the Very Worshipful...............................

Grand Secretary of the Grand Lodge of Nevada:—

I hereby certify that Brother................., who died at............,
on the......day of........., A. L. 58..., was at the date of his decease,

a Master Mason and a member of this Lodge, in good standing; and that he left (*here insert " a widow," " a child," or " children," or any of them, as the case may be,*) for whose benefit a Grand Lodge Diploma is desired.

Given by order of the Lodge aforesaid, at the date first
[Seal.]   above written, as witness my hand and Seal thereof.
....*Secretary.*

FORM *of a Petition for a Dispensation to form a new Lodge.*
To the Most Worshipful.....................................
Grand Master of Masons in Nevada:—

The petition of the undersigned respectfully represents that they are Master Masons in good standing; that they were last members of the respective Lodges named opposite their several signatures hereunto, as will appear from the dimits of each of the petitioners, herewith transmitted; that they reside in or near the............of...............in the county of............, in the State of Nevada; that among them are a sufficient number of brethren well qualified to open and hold a Lodge of Free and Accepted Masons, and to discharge all its various duties in the three degrees of Ancient Masonry, in accordance with established usage; and that, having the prosperity of the Craft at heart, and being desirous to use their best endeavors for the diffusion of its beneficent principles, they pray for a Dispensation empowering them to form, open, and hold a regular Lodge at the............of............, aforesaid, to be called.................Lodge.

They have nominated, and respectfully recommend Brother ....as the first Master, Brother...............as the first Senior Warden, and Brother...............as the first Junior Warden of the said Lodge, they being in all respects competent to perform all the duties of the several stations for which they are proposed; and, if the prayer of the petitioners be granted, they promise in all things strict obedience to the commands of the Grand Master, and undeviating conformity to the Constitution and Regulations of the Grand Lodge.

Dated at...................., on the......day of...............A. L. 58...

SIGNATURES.	NAME AND NO. OF LODGE.	STATE OR COUNTY.

FORM *of Recommendation of a Petition for the institution of a New Lodge.*

.....................Lodge, No......., F. and M., ⎱
....................................., A. L., 58... ⎰
To the Most Worshipful.....................................
Grand Master of Masons in Nevada:—

At a stated communication of this Lodge, held at the date above written, the following preamble and resolution were adopted :—

"WHEREAS, a petition for the issue af a Dispensation to form and open a new Lodge at.................., in the county of.............., has been presented to this Lodge for its recommendation ; *And Whereas*, it is known to this Lodge that the signers to said petition, ...in number, are all Master Masons in good standing, and that a safe and suitable Lodge-room has been provided by them for their meetings ; it is

"*Resolved*, That the establishment of said new Lodge is of manifest propriety, and will conduce to the good of the Order ; and that this Lodge recommends to the Grand Master the granting of the Dispensation prayed for in said petition."

A true copy from the minutes.

[Seal.] In testimony whereof I have hereunto set my hand and affixed the Seal of the Lodge aforesaid, at the date above written.

....*Secretary.*

FORM *of Certificate of the qualifications of the Master proposed in a Petition for a New Lodge.*

To the Most Worshipful..................................

Grand Master of Masons in Nevada :—

The petition of......brethren, residing at the.........of........., in the county of..........:praying the Grand Master for a Dispensation to open and hold a new Lodge at said............, to be called.......... Lodge, having been presented to me ; and Brother..............being recommended therein for nomination as the first Master of said proposed new Lodge ; now, I..............Master of..............Lodge, No......., do hereby certify that, to my positive knowledge, said Brother..............is fully competent properly to confer the three degrees of Masonry, and to deliver entire the several lectures thereunto appertaining.

Given at.............., in the county of...........this...:........day of.............., A. L. 58.

....*Master.*

FORM *of Petition for a Charter.*

To the M∴W∴Grand Lodge of Nevada :—

The undersigned respectfully represent that on the......day of............, A. L. 58..., a Dispensation was issued by the Grand Master for the formation of a new Lodge at............in the county

of............., by the name of...:.........Lodge ; that on the..........day
of.............next ensuing, said Lodge was opened and organized, and
has since continued successfully to work during the period named
in said Dispensation, as will appear from its records, by-laws and
returns, herewith presented ; and that it is the anxious desire of
the members of said Lodge that its existence be perpetuated.

They therefore pray that a charter be granted to said Lodge, by
the name of...................Lodge, with such number as the usage of
the Grand Lodge may assign it ; and recommend that Brother
.................be named therein as Master, Brother...................as
Senior Warden, and Brother...................... as Junior Warden ;
promising as heretofore, strict obedience to the commands of the
Grand Master, and undeviating conformity to the Constitution and
Regulations of the Grand Lodge.

Given by instruction from, and on behalf of said Lodge, at......
this.........day of................A. L., 58...

> ....
> .... } Delegates.
> ....

FORM *of Credentials as Representatives elected by a Lodge.*

.................Lodge No.......F. and A. M., }
....A. L. 58... }

To the M.·.W.·.Grand Lodge of Nevada :—

This is to certify that at a...............Communication of this
Lodge, held at the date above written, it having been made known
that neither the Master nor either of the Wardens thereof would be
entitled to attend the Grand Lodge at its next Annual Communication, Bro....................a member of the Lodge, was, by ballot,
duly elected to serve as Representative during said Grand Communication.

[Seal.]   In testimony whereof I have hereunto set my hand
and have caused the Secretary to affix the Seal of
the Lodge, with his attestation, at the date above
written.

.............................Master.

...........................Secretary.

FORM *of Petition for the Degrees of Masonry.*

To the Worshipful Master, Wardens and members of

..........................Lodge No......, F. and A. M. :—

The undersigned respectfully represents, that, unbiassed by

friends, and uninfluenced by mercenary motives, he freely and voluntarily offers himself as a candidate for the mysteries of Masonry : that he is prompted to solicit this privilege by a favorable opinion conceived of the institution, a desire for knowledge, and a sincere wish to be serviceable to his fellow creatures ; that he has resided in the State of Nevada more than one year, and at the place below named more than six months next preceding the date hereof ; that he has not, within twelve months past, been rejected by any Lodge of Free and Accepted Masons ; and that he promises if found worthy, to conform to all the ancient usages and regulations of the Fraternity.

His place of residence is................, his age,........... ....years, and his occupation......................

(*Date*,)............................., 18.....

(*Signature,*)................................

Recommended by Bros. $\left\{ \begin{array}{c} .... \\ (\textit{To be Members of the Lodge.}) \\ .... \end{array} \right.$

FORM *of Application for Membership.*

To the Worshipful Master, Wardens, and Brethren of ....Lodge, No......., F. and A. M. :—

The undersigned respectfully represents, that he is a Master Mason, in good standing; that he was last a member of.............. Lodge, No......., in the............of..................., from which he has honorably withdrawn, as by the accompanying certificate will appear, and that he now desires, if found worthy, to become a member of your Lodge.

His place of residence is..................., his age................... years, and his occupation............................

(*Date*,)............... ....A. L., 58...

Signature,)...........................

Recommended by Bros. $\left\{ \begin{array}{c} .... \\ (\textit{To be Members of the Lodge.}) \\ .... \end{array} \right.$

FORM *of Certificate of the election and installation of the Officers of a Subordinate Lodge.*

...............................Lodge, No......., F. and A. M. }
...............................A. L. 58... }

To the Very Worshipful.............................

Grand Secretary of the Grand Lodge of Nevada :—
I hereby certify that, at the stated Communication of this Lodge, held on the day above written, it being the next preceding

the anniversary of St. John the Evangelist, the following officers were duly elected for the ensuing Masonic year, viz:—

Bro..............................., Master.
Bro..............................., Sen. Warden.
Bro..............................., Jun. Warden.
Bro..............................., Treasurer.
Bro..............................., Secretary.

And that on the.........day of............A. L. 58..., said officers were duly installed by (*here give the name and Masonic title of the installing Officer.*)

[Seal.]   Given under my hand and the Seal of the Lodge, on the day last above written.

.....:..............................Secretary.

FORM *of Notice of Rejections, Suspensions, Expulsions, and Restorations.*

..........................Lodge, No......., F. and A. M. ⎫
....A. L. 58... ⎭

To the Very Worshipful..................................
  Grand Secretary of the Grand Lodge of Nevada:—

  I hereby certify that, at a stated Communication of this Lodge held at the date above written, the petition of......................, an applicant for the degrees of Masonry was rejected.

  (*Or*, Bro....................., after due notice, as prescribed in the Constitution, was suspended from all the rights and privileges of Masonry, for non-payment of his dues.)

  (*Or*, Bro....................., after due trial in the manner prescribed in the Constitution, was declared to be suspended from all the rights and privileges of Masonry, for unmasonic conduct.)

  (*Or*, Bro....................., after due trial, in the manner prescribed in the Constitution, was declared to be expelled from all the rights and privileges of Masonry, for unmasonic conduct.)

  (*Or*, Bro....................., heretofore suspended by this Lodge for non-payment of his dues, having paid up all arrearages, (or, having had his dues remitted by the Lodge,) as provided in the Constitution, resumed his rights and privileges as a Mason and as a member of this Lodge.)

  (*Or*, Bro....................., heretofore suspended by this Lodge for unmasonic conduct, was, by a two-thirds vote, in the manner prescribed in the Constititution, restored to all his rights and privileges as a Mason, and as a member of this Lodge.)

[Seal.]   Given under my hand and the Seal of the Lodge aforesaid, at the date above written.

..................................Secretary.

General Regulations,

ADOPTED JANUARY 18, A. L. 5865.

1. The practice of duelling being repugnant to the principles of Freeasonry, in all cases where two brethren resort to this mode of settling their disputes, it shall be the duty of the Lodge or Lodges of which they are members, or within whose jurisdiction they may reside, forthwith to expel them from all the rights and privileges of Masonry ; and no brother who may fall in a duel shall be buried with Masonic honors.

2. All bodies purporting to be Masonic Lodges, held in the United States or any of their Territories, within the jurisdiction of the Grand Lodge of any State or Territory, without authority from such Grand Lodge, and all the members thereof, are declared illegal.

3. All Lodges within this State, having concurrent jurisdiction with other Lodges, shall immediately notify such others of all applications for membership or initiation.

4. This Grand Lodge, recognizing the principle that no one should be initiated into the mysteries of our Order, except in the Lodge nearest his place of residence, (unless by its permission,) and, while it takes care to avoid infringing the jurisdictional rights of others, will not tolerate that its own be invaded ; and it is therefore ordered that no Lodge, subordinate to the Grand Lodge of Nevada, shall admit to membership any person who, being at the time a resident of this State, has received, or claims to have received the degrees of Masonry from any source beyond its jurisdiction, without the proper permission, until he shall have paid the Lodge to which he applies for membership, the full amount charged by that Lodge for conferring the degrees, less the sum paid by him to the Lodge in which he received them.

5. All Masonic communication between the Lodges and Masons of this jurisdiction and those acknowledging allegiance to the Grand Lodge of Hamburg, is hereby forbidden, while that body shall continue its unlawful and reprehensible invasion of the jurisdictional rights of the Grand Lodge of New York.

6. This Grand Lodge recognizes no *degree* of Past Master conferred by any authority not holden under a legitimate Grand Lodge —acknowledging only the order of that name as it exists in the ceremonies attending the installation of the Master elect of a chartered Lodge : which order shall be conferred only by a convocation of Present or Past Masters, not less than three in number, who have thus regularly received it.

7. No Lodge ynder this jurisdiction, shall be allowed to transact business, other than the conferring of degrees, with a less number than seven members present.

8. The Grand Secretary is authorized to charge the sum of one dollar, for the use of the Grand Lodge, for each copy of its printed proceedings for the current year, other than the four copies to be sent to each subordinate Lodge, and those required for transmission abroad, for future binding, and for the use of the Grand Lodge at its next succeeding Annual Communication.

9. When a brother, found guilty of a Masonic offense and sentenced to be reprimanded, appeals from the verdict and sentence, such sentence shall not be carried into effect until the appeal shall have been disposed of by the Grand Lodge,

10. The names of entered Apprentices and Fellow Crafts shall be returned to the Grand Lodge for two years only, and shall thereafter be dropped from the rolls of their respective Lodges.

11. Non-affiiliated Masons, who are suspended by operation of Sec. 1, Art. II, Part V, of the Constitution, if they desire to restore themselves either by affiliation or contribution, shall pay a sum equal to six months dues, in addition to the affiliation fee, or a sum equal to the dues of the Lodge, for all the time they have resided in the jurisdiction of the Lodge unaffiliated, unless sickness or inabilty be shown as the reason for non-affiliation or non-payment.

12. All non-affiliated Masons, within the jurisdiction of this Grand Lodge, shall be warned and notified to present themselves at the nearest Lodge to their place of abode, and affiliate with said Lodge, unless for cause shown they shall be excused by said Lodge.

All Masons in this jurisdiction, who after having been faithfully and fully warned, shall fail or refuse to appear as herein required, or appearing, refuse to affiliate or show cause for non-affiliation, shall be deemed unworthy of and denied all Masonic privileges, rights and charities, unless they produce a certificate from the Secretary of the Lodge, or the Secretary of the Masonic Board of Relief, within whose Jurisdiction they reside, or from the Grand Secretary, that they have contributed to such Lodge, Board of Relief, or this Grand Lodge, an amount equivalent to the dues of such Lodge. .

INDEX

OF

Constitution and Regulations.

———◆◆◆———

Funeral Service.

No Mason can be interred with the formalities of the Order, unless he shall have been raised to the Third Degree. Fellow Crafts and Entered Apprentices are not entitled to Masonic obsequies, nor can they join in processions on such occasions.

All brethren in attendance at a funeral should be decently clothed in black, with crape on left arm, and with white gloves and aprons.

The brethren having assembled at the Lodge-room, the Master opens the Lodge in the Third degree of Masonry, states the purpose for which it has been called together, and calls the Lodge off.

The service is then commenced as follows :—

Master. What man is he that liveth and shall not see death? Shall he deliver his soul from the hand of the grave ?

Response. Man walketh in a vain shadow; he heapeth up riches and cannot tell who shall gather them.

Master. When he dieth he shall carry nothing away ; his glory shall not descend after him.

Response. Naked came he into the world, and naked must he return. The Lord gave and the Lord hath taken away ; blessed be the name of the Lord.

Master. If a man die shall he live again?

Response. The dust shall return to the earth as it was ; and the spirit shall return to God who gave it.

Master. Can we offer no precious offering to redeem our lost brother ?

Response. We have not the ransom ; the place that knew him once, shall know him no more forever.

Master. Shall his name be lost upon earth?

Response. We will record it in our hearts, we will treasure it in our memories, being dead he shall yet speak to us, in the recollection of his virtues.

Master. Our brother has fulfilled his earthly destiny ; may we all live the life of the righteous, that our last end may be like his.

Response. God is our God for ever and ever ! may he be our guide even unto death.

Master. Almighty Father ! in thy hands we leave with humble submission the soul of our deceased brother.

Response. (*Repeated three times, giving the grand honors each time.*) The will of God is accomplished. So mote it be. Amen.

Master. Brethren, let us here drop the tear of sorrow at the loss of our departed brother who shall meet us no more in the mysteries and fellowship of our beloved order. Let us keep fresh in our memories his virtues, and strive to imitate them. Let us cast about his infirmities, whatever they may have been, the broad mantle of a Mason's charity, remembering that it is human to err, but divine, to forgive what is evil and to love that which is good.

Master or Chaplain. Oh! Father of mercies and God of all comfort, our only help in time of need, look with pity, we pray thee, upon the sorrows of thy servants, and sanctify to us Thy fatherly correction. Make us deeply sensible of the shortness and uncertainty of human life. So teach us to number our days, that we may apply our hearts unto wisdom. Let Thy Holy Spirit lead us through this vale of misery, in holiness and righteousness all the days of our lives. When Thou shall call us hence may we depart, having the testimony of good conscience; in the confidence of a certain faith; in the comfort of a reasonable, religious, and holy hope; in favor with Thee our God, and in perfect charity with the world; may we pass from this earthly Lodge of sorrow to Thy joyful House not made with hands, eternal in the heavens. Amen.

Response. So mote it be.

Solemn music may here be introduced.

The procession shall then be formed. If the body be not in the Lodge-room, the procession will move to the house of the deceased, and thence with his remains to the place of sepulchre, in the following order :

The Tyler with a drawn sword ;

Stewards, with white Rods ;

Musicians,

(If Masons ; otherwise they will follow the Tyer ;)

Master Masons ;

Junior and Senior Deacons ;

Secretary and Treasurer ;

Junior and Senior Wardens :

Past Masters ;

The Holy Writings;

On a cushion covered with black cloth, carried by the oldest member of the Lodge ;

The Master ;

The Reverend Clergy ;

The   Body,

With the insignia   placed thereon ;

Pall bearers ;   Pall bearers;

Mourners.

When the procession arrives within a proper distance of the grave, the brethren will halt, open out right and left and face inwards, to allow the latter part of the procession to pass through in the following order:

Chaplain or officiating Clergyman;
Coffin ;
Mourners ;
Worshipful Master;
Brethren in reversed order ;

On arriving at the grave the brethren form a circle around it, the officers and Reverend Clergy at the head, the mourners at the foot. The regalia is taken from the coffin by the Senior Deacon, and the coffin deposited in the grave. After the Clergyman has concluded the religious services of the Church, the Worshipful Master shall proceed as follows :

Master. My brethren: here, about this open grave, has the solemn voice of our Heavenly Father again called us to stand, that we may tenderly lay the lifeless body of our departed brother in the long home, and take to our hearts the solemn message that thither every man goeth.

To us who remain, death seems far off. How often is our inward thought that our houses shall continue forever, and our dwelling places to all generations ; so we call lands after our own names, heap up riches, and go on as if we are to live forever, and not see corruption. But this grave tells us that we too will soon pass hence, and leave behind us all that is of the earth, earthy ; then will we enter into the world beyond where all things are eternal, and what is now unseen becomes visible. The world passeth away, and the lust thereof ; but he that doeth the will of God, abideth forever. Let us then henceforth rightly divide our time, and apply our hearts unto the divine wisdom, that we may stand in our everlasting lot at the end of the days.

The following invocations are then rehearsed by the Master, and responded to by the brethren.

Master May we be true and faithful, and may we live and die in love !

Response. So mote it be.

Master. May we profess only that which is good, and may we always act in accordance with our professions !

Response. So mote it be.

Master. May the Lord bless us and prosper us, and may all our good intentions be crowned with success !

Response. So mote it be.

The Senior Deacon then hands the Master the Apron, and the Master continues :

This Lamb-skin, or white apron, is an emblem of innocence, and the peculiar badge of a Mason. It is more ancient than the Golden Fleece or Roman Eagle, and, when worthily worn, more honorable than Star or Garter, or any other order which earthly power can confer. Being the Badge of Innocence and the Bond of

Friendship, this emblem which we now deposit in the grave of our deceased brother, (*drops it in the grave*,) reminds us that the dominion of death is universal; that the wealth of the world cannot buy or release, and that neither the strong arm of friendship nor the virtue of innocence can prevent his coming.

The Master, holding the evergreen in his hand, continues:

This evergreen is an emblem of our faith in the immortality of our souls, which the grave shall never receive, over which death hath no dominion, and which shall pass through the valley of the shadow of death to its eternal destiny beyond. "For we know that our Redeemer liveth, and that he shall stand at the latter day upon the earth."

A Funeral Dirge may then be sung or played while the brethren move in procession around the grave, each depositing in it a sprig of evergreen as he passes the head. The Secretary then drops his roll upon the coffin; and the public Grand Honors are given thrice, all repeating at each time:—

The will of God is accomplished! So mote it be! Amen!

The cover is then placed on the outer case. The Master then continues as follows:

Brother, we commit thy body to the grave; earth to earth, (*here the Senior Deacon drops earth on the coffin three several times,*) ashes to ashes, dust to dust. We bid thee a long, a last farewell; thine earthly toil is over; mayest thou rest forever in heavenly peace. Amen.

Response. So mote it be.

BRETHREN AND FRIENDS:—From time immemorial it has been the custom among the Fraternity of Free and Accepted Masons, at the request of a Brother, to accompany his remains to the place of interment, and there to deposit them with the usual formalities of the Craft. In conformity to this usage and at the desire of our deceased brother, whose loss we deplore and whose memory we revere, we have assembled in the character of Masons to resign his body to the earth, whence it came, and to offer up to his memory before the world this last tribute of affection; thereby demonstrating the sincerity of our esteem for him, and our unchanging attachment to the principles of our Order.

Our departed brother's course on the level of time has ended; we are speedily after him to reach the same bound appointed us of God which we may not pass. The Grand Master has called from earthly toil one of his workmen to apply to him and his work the square of righteous judgment. Before that august Master, in the Lodge of Eternity, we also must shortly appear, and submit our work for inspection. Let us then work while it is day; encourage and help one another; take the Holy Scriptures as the rule and guide of our faith and practice; and heartily make ready to be raised at the divine call to the heavenly kingdom which has been prepared for faithful Craftsmen.

Response. So mote it be.

W.·.M.·.or Chaplain. Almighty and most merciful God, in whom we live and move, and have our being, and before whom all men must appear to give an account of the deeds done in the body, have mercy upon us. Convince our minds and teach our hearts by the solemn lessons of this day.

Vouschafe us, we pray Thee, Thy divine assistance to redeem our mispent time, and to build aright, in the days which remain, our spiritual edifice. Give us wisdom from on high to direct us; strength to support us; the beauty of holiness to adorn our lives. At last, when the gavel of Death shall call us from our labors, may we enter into the blessed and everlasting rest of the kingdom above. Amen.

Response. So mote it be.

The Master then approaches the head of the grave and says :—

Soft and safe be this the earthly bed of our brother. Bright and glorious be his rising from it! Fragrant be the cassia sprig that here shall flourish! May the earliest buds of spring unfold their beauties o'er this his resting place. Though the cold blasts of autumn may lay them in the dust, and for a time destroy the loveliness of their existence, yet the destruction is not final, and in the spring they shall surely bloom again. So, in the bright morning of the world's resurrection, his mortal frame now laid in the dust by the chilling blast of Death, may spring again into newness of life, and expand, in immortal beauty, in realms beyond the skies.

(*Benediction.*) The Lord bless us and keep us—the Lord make his face to shine upon us, and be gracious unto us—the Lord lift upon us the light of his countenance, and give us peace,

Response. Amen! So mote it be.

Thus the services end. The procession will reform and return to the Lodge-room, and the Lodge will be closed in the customary manner.

FUNERAL DIRGE.

AIR, *Pleyel's German Hymn.*

1 *Solemn strikes the fun'ral chime,*
 Notes of our departing time ;
 As we journey here below,
 Through a pilgrimage of woe.

2 Mortals, now indulge a tear,
 For mortality is here ;
 See how wide her trophies wave
 O'er the slumbers of the grave.

3 *Here, another Guest we bring !*
 Seraphs, of celestial wing,
 To our fun'ral altar come ;
 Waft a Friend and Brother home.

4 Far beyond the grave, there lie
 Brighter mansions in the sky ;
 Where, enthroned, the Deity
 Gives man immortality.

5 There, enlarged, his soul will see
 What was veiled in mystery ;
 Heavenly glories of the place
 Show his Maker " face to face."

6 God of Life's ETERNAL DAY !
 Guide us, lest from Thee we stray,
 By a false, delusive light,
 To the shades of endless night.

7 Calm, the GOOD MAN meets his fate ;
 Guards celestial round him wait !
 See ; he bursts these mortal chains,
 And o'er Death the vict'ry gains !

8 *Lord of all below, above,*
 Fill our souls with Truth and Love ;
 As dissolves our Earthly Tie,
 Take us to thy LODGE on HIGH !

NOTE.—It is customary to sing only the 1st, 3d, and 8th stanzas. On funeral occasions the first two of these may be sung on entering the burial-ground, while moving in procession ; and the last during the ceremonies at the grave.

BY-LAWS

OF

Elko Lodge, No. 15,

F. & A. M.

ARTICLE I.

OF NAME AND OFFICERS.

SECTION 1. This Lodge shall be known by the name of ELKO Lodge, No. 15, of Free and Accepted Masons, and its officers shall consist of a Master, a Senior Warden, a Junior Warden, a Treasurer, a Secretary, a Senior Deacon, a Junior Deacon, a Marshal, two Stewards, a Tyler, and such other officers as the Lodge may deem proper to appoint.

ARTICLE II.

OF ELECTIONS AND APPOINTMENTS.

SECTION 1. The Master, the Senior Warden, the Junior Warden, the Treasurer and the Secretary, shall be elected by ballot, in conformity with Sec. 1, Art. 1, Part IV, of the Constitution of the Grand Lodge. The other officers shall be appointed by the Master, except the Junior Deacon, who may be appointed by the Senior Warden.

ARTICLE III.

OF COMMUNICATIONS OF THE LODGE.

SECTION 1. The stated Communications of the Lodge shall be holden on the first Tuesday in each month.

SEC. 2. Special Communications may be called from time to time, as the Lodge or the presiding officer thereof may direct.

ARTICLE IV.

OF INITIATION AND MEBERSHIP.

SECTION 1. All petitions for initiation or affiliation must be signed by the petitioner, and be recommended by two members of the Lodge, and accompanied with the usual fee. · Every such petition shall be referred to a committee of three, whose duty it shall be to report thereon, at the next stated Communication, (unless further time be granted) when the applicant may be balloted for, and received or rejected, or the ballot may be postponed until the ensuing stated Communication, as the Lodge may determine.

SEC. 2. If an applicant elected to receive the degrees in this Lodge, does not come forward to be initiated within three months thereafter, the fee shall be forfeited unless the Lodge shall otherwise direct.

SEC. 3. Every person raised to the degree of Master Mason in, or elected a member of this Lodge, shall sign the By-Laws thereof.

ARTICLE V.

.OF THE TREASURER.

SECTION 1. The Treasurer shall receive all moneys from the Secretary ; shall keep an accurate and just account thereof, and shall pay the same out only upon an order duly signed by the Master, and countersigned by the Secretary. He shall at the stated Communications in December, March, June and September of each year, submit a report in full of the monetary transactions of the Lodge. The Lodge may also, at any time when considered necessary, cause him to present an account of his receipts and disbursements, and of the amount of funds on hand.

ARTICLE VI.

OF THE SECRETARY.

SECTION 1. The Secretary shall keep a faithful record of all proceedings proper to be written ; shall transmit a copy of the same to the Grand Lodge when required ; shall keep a separate account for each member of the Lodge ; shall report at the stated Communications in December, March, June and September, the amount due by each member ; shall receive all moneys due the Lodge, and pay the same to the Treasurer ; and shall perform all such other duties as may properly appertain to his office.

SEC. 2. He shall receive such compensation for his services as the Lodge may direct.

ARTICLE VII.

OF THE TYLER.

SECTION 1. The Tyler, in addition to the necessary duties of his office, shall serve all notices and summonses, and perform such other services as may be required of him by the Lodge.

SEC. 2. He shall receive as compensation for his services, Two Dollars for each Communication of the Lodge.

ARTICLE VIII.

SECTION 1. The table of fees for this Lodge shall be as follows: For the degree of Entered Apprentice, $25; for the degree of Fellow Craft, $20; for the degree of Master Mason, $30.

ARTICLE IX.

OF DUES.

SECTION 1. The dues of each Member of this Lodge shall be One Dollar per month, payable quarterly.

SEC. 2. No member who is six months in arrears for dues at the time of Annual Election, shall be permitted to vote, or shall be eligible to any office.

SEC. 3. Any member, who has been suspended for non-payment of his dues, may be restored to membership upon payment of all arrearages.

SEC. 4. Any member in good standing may withdraw from membership by paying his dues and notifying the Lodge to that effect, at a stated Communication, but no recommendatory certificate shall be issued unless ordered by the Lodge.

ARTICLE X.

OF COMMITTEES.

SECTION 1. The Master and Wardens shall be a charity committee, and shall have power to draw upon the Treasurer for any sum not exceeding ten dollars, at any one time, for the relief of a distressed worthy brother, his wife, widow or orphans.

SEC. 2. The Master and Wardens shall constitute an Auditing Committee, whose duty it shall be to examine all accounts presented against the Lodge.

SEC. 3. All reports of committees shall be made in writing.

ARTICLE XI.

OF WIDOWS AND ORPHANS FUND.

SECTION 1. The fees received by the Lodge for every degree of

Master Mason conferred herein, shall be set apart by the Treasurer to the credit of the Widow's and Orphan's Fund.

Sec. 2 The Masters and Wardens shall be Trustees of the Widows and Orphan's Fund, and shall have full control of the same, with power to invest it on good security.

Sec. 3. All interest accruing to said fund shall be added to the principal, until the fund amounts to five hundred dollars and over. The Trustees may then draw upon it for the relief of Widows or Orphans under the care of the Lodge; provided, that at no time shall the said fund be drawn upon so as to leave less than two hundred dollars therein.

ARTICLE XII.

OF REVEALING THE TRANSACTIONS OF THE LODGE.

Section 1. When a candidate for initiation or affiliation is rejected, or a brother reprimanded, suspended, or expelled, no member or visitor shall reveal, either directly or indirectly, to such person, or to any other, any transactions which may have taken place on the subject, nor shall any proceedings of the Lodge not proper to be made public be disclosed outside thereof, under the penalty of reprimand or expulsion, as the Lodge may determine.

ARTICLE XIII.

OF ORDER OF BUSINESS.

Section 1. The regular order of business at every stated Communication of the Lodge, shall be as follows:—
1. Reading of the Minutes.
2. Reports of Commitees.
3. Ballotings.
4. Reception of Petitions.
5. Miscellaneous and Unfinished Business.
6. Conferring Degrees.

ARTICLE XIV.

OF AMENDMENTS.

Section 1. These By-Laws may be amended at any stated Commuication, by a vote of two-thirds of the members present; provided that notice of such amendment shall have been given at the stated Communication next preceding, but such amendment shall have no effect until approved by the Grand Lodge or Grand Master, and until such approval shall have been transmitted to the Grand Secretary.

OFFICERS AND MEMBERS

OF

Elko Lodge, No. 15, F. & A. M.

MARCH 5, 1872.

Jonah D. Treat, *Master.*
Elijah S. Yeates, *Senior Warden.*
Otto Frilling, *Junior Warden.*
Robert Oliver, *Treasurer.*
Thomas N. Stone, *Secretary.*

William Plughoff, *Senior Deacon.*
Antoni Bixel, *Junior Deacon.*
C. R. VanAelstyn, } *Stewards.*
Geo. B. Kittridge, } *Stewards.*
Walter Chase, *Tyler.*

MASTER MASONS.

Alexander, Jacob.
Abel, G. B.
Burkett, John P.
Bennett, William M.
Brewster, George P.
Carpeaux, Edmond J.
Cassen, James.
Dyer, William F.
Ellis, John J.
Eichnauer, John C.
Fisher, Allen.
Free, Franklin.
Freeman, Merrill P.
Garrecht, Theobald.
Hoffman, J. J.
Henly, Thomas B.
Holmes, Thomas.
Hamill, Thomas.
Harenor, William M.
Hamlyn, Thomas.
Hale, Charles H.

Jenkins, Samuel K.
Kenyon, Thomas C.
Leventhall, Edward.
Lawson, Walter.
Lucas, John H.
McDermitt, James.
McMullen, Samuel.
McBurney, James.
O'Connor, Thomas.
Reinhart, Simon.
Stafford, William M.
Speilman, A.
Seitz, George.
Sargent, Bejamin F.
Smith, Albert J.
Smith, Wellington T.
Tobias, A. J.
Urton, W. J.
VanDreilin, W. Smith
Wines, Leonard.
Waterman, Thomas A.

Woodworth, J. M.